There are many good books that offer Christians wise words of caution about the role of technology in our lives, but *Redeeming Technology* goes beyond that by offering practical suggestions on how our approach to and use of technology can be a beautiful expression of our love for God and the many neighbors in our lives. This book is a great source of personal learning and also an excellent resource for small group study and discussion.

Bernard Bull, president of Concordia University Nebraska

A psychiatrist and a pastor tell us about the mental and spiritual effects of technology. They do so in a lively and eye-opening book full of research, anecdotes, and lore. While showing that technology changes us in some harmful ways, Rev. Sutton and Dr. Smith are not digital Luddites. Rather, they show us how—through the Gospel—we can break our addictions to the misuse of technology and use it for good.

Gene Edward Veith Jr., author of *Spirituality of the Cross*

Redeeming Technology is all about Jesus. Sutton and Smith unpack a Christ-centered view about technology and explore diverse connections to the Scriptures, without ignoring health science. The text ranges from literature to biblical case studies, allowing the reader to interact with unique insights and construct a healthier use of digital technology. In this sense, *Redeeming Technology* invites us to regard technology as part of the human plot of creation, fall, and redemption.

Rev. Mário Rafael Fukue, chaplain at ULBRA-Brasil
and professor at Seminário Concórdia, Brasil

The negative impact of our society's addiction to digital media is ubiquitous in our homes, schools, and even our churches. In response to this, Rev. Sutton and Dr. Smith have written a book that is exceedingly well researched, engaging, and even inspirational. A practical guide to dealing with digital media using a God-centered approach, it should be required reading for Christian parents of children of all ages.

Dr. Anthony Youn, best-selling author of *The Age Fix*,
physician, and social media influencer

REDEEMING TECHNOLOGY

A Christian Approach to Healthy Digital Habits

A. Trevor Sutton | Brian Smith, MD

CONCORDIA PUBLISHING HOUSE • SAINT LOUIS

Published by Concordia Publishing House
3558 S. Jefferson Avenue, St. Louis, MO 63118-3968
1-800-325-3040 • cph.org

Manufactured in the United States of America

Library of Congress Cataloging-in-Publication Data
Names: Sutton, A. Trevor, author. | Smith, Brian, co-author.
Title: Redeeming technology : a Christian approach to healthy digital habits / A. Trevor Sutton and co-author Brian Smith.
Description: Saint Louis, MO : Concordia Publishing House, [2021]
Identifiers: LCCN 2021020626 (print) | LCCN 2021020627 (ebook) | ISBN 9780758669957 (paperback) | ISBN 9780758669964 (ebook)
Subjects: LCSH: Technology--Religious aspects--Christianity. | Digital media--Religious aspects--Christianity. | Habit breaking--Religious aspects--Christianity.
Classification: LCC BR115.T42 S88 2021 (print) | LCC BR115.T42 (ebook) | DDC 261.5/6--dc23
LC record available at https://lccn.loc.gov/2021020626
LC ebook record available at https://lccn.loc.gov/2021020627

1 2 3 4 5 6 7 8 9 10   30 29 28 27 26 25 24 23 22 21

DEDICATION

Bill and Gwen and Pete and Jennifer
—A. Trevor Sutton

Sara, Brandon, Hannah, Casey, and Chewie
—Brian Smith

CONTENTS

ACKNOWLEDGMENTS

> May the God of endurance and encouragement grant you to live in such harmony with one another, in accord with Christ Jesus, that together you may with one voice glorify the God and Father of our Lord Jesus Christ.
>
> Romans 15:5–6

Writing a book has its challenges. Writing a book together as a team can be particularly challenging. Oftentimes, co-authored projects are an awkward *pas de deux* with the authors stepping on each other's words and tripping over each other's ideas.

Not this one. By the grace of God and the presence of the Holy Spirit, this book came together with great harmony and unity so that it was a joy to write. Therefore, we want to give all glory to God for the spirit of peace and accord that pervaded throughout this collaboration.

Additionally, we greatly appreciate and want to acknowledge many others.

Brian (Dr. Smith) would like to thank his wife, Sara, as well as his sons, Brandon and Casey, and daughter, Hannah, for their love, laughs, and togetherness during times of joy and challenge. He would like to acknowledge his parents, Jerry and Deborah, for their invaluable support, including encouraging his writing. He would also like to thank everyone associated with the Michigan State University Department of Psychiatry—

patients, colleagues, residents, students, and staff—for transforming psychiatry from a job into a calling. Finally, Dr. Anthony Youn deserves special mention for decades of collaboration and friendship.

Trevor would like to acknowledge his wife, Elizabeth, as well as his daughters, Grace and Hannah, for their love and prayers. He would also like to thank the people of St. Luke Lutheran Church (Meridian Township and Lansing, Michigan) and his colleagues at Michigan State University and Concordia Seminary. Additionally, he would like to express his gratitude to Dave Davis and Trevin Wax for modeling purposeful and constructive uses of social media and technology. Many others are not listed by name but are fully deserving of his appreciation.

Finally, we would like to thank Laura Lane, Jamie Moldenhauer, and the rest of the team at Concordia Publishing House for their guidance and editorial wisdom. We are also thankful for the late Rev. Paul T. McCain for his enthusiasm and support for this project when we first began discussing it. This book would never have happened without the wisdom, support, and encouragement of all these individuals.

To God be the glory!

FIGURE 1. Gulliver holding his pocket watch. Image from Jonathan Swift, *Gulliver's Travels*, ed. Thomas M. Balliet (Boston: D. C. Heath and Co., 1900), Project Gutenberg, November 26, 2005, http://www.gutenberg.org/files/17157/17157-h/17157-h .htm.

CHAPTER 1

INVISIBLE CORDS

Lemuel Gulliver was addicted to technology. Binge-watching shows on Netflix was not his drug of choice. Facebook, Instagram, and Twitter did not fuel his cravings. And he had no interest in online gaming.

No, Lemuel was addicted to his pocket watch.

This tale of technology addiction comes from *Gulliver's Travels*. Written by Jonathan Swift in the eighteenth century, this fictional tale takes place in part on the strange island of Lilliput. When Lemuel landed upon the shores of Lilliput, the miniature inhabitants of the island studied him with great fascination. The Lilliputians knew nothing of who he was, where he had come from, or what made him tick.

So they observed everything he did. The emperor made a careful survey of this great man-mountain. The aristocrats marveled at how he could consume thirty wagons full of food. And military officers took a careful inventory of his personal items.

Among Lemuel's personal items was a pocket watch. Observing his incessant interactions with this pocket watch, the Lilliputians described his technology addiction as bordering on religious devotion: "We conjecture it is either some unknown animal, *or the god that he worships*; but we are more inclined to

FIGURE 2. The Lilliputians inspect the pocket watch. Image from Jonathan Swift, *Gulliver's Travels*, ed. Thomas M. Balliet (Boston: D. C. Heath and Co., 1900), Project Gutenberg, November 26, 2005, http://www.gutenberg.org/files/17157/17157 -h/17157-h.htm.

the latter opinion, because he assured us . . . that he seldom did anything without consulting it."[1]

Watching Lemuel interact with this piece of technology, the Lilliputians concluded that it must be his god. He seemed to worship it. Upon waking in the morning, he would check it. Before having a meal, he would consult it. During a conversation, he would confer with it. When he was bored, he would reach for it. This pocket watch was the first thing he saw in the morning and the last thing he looked at before closing his eyes at the end of the day.

---

1   Jonathan Swift, *Gulliver's Travels*, ed. Thomas M. Balliet (Boston: D. C. Heath and Co., 1900), part 1, chapter 2, Project Gutenberg, November 26, 2005, http://www.gutenberg .org/files/17157/17157-h/17157-h.htm, emphasis added.

His pocket watch—or maybe it really was the god that he worshiped—was an omnipresent part of his daily life.

WHEN FICTION BECOMES REALITY

This fictional tale has become a reality for many of us. Were the Lilliputians to observe us, they would surely conclude that technology is the god we worship. Lemuel Gulliver's adoration of his pocket watch was lilliputian compared to our devotion to modern technology.

On average, we check our phones nearly 100 times per day.[2] Some sources place it even higher! The average American devotes eleven hours of the day to staring at glowing rectangles and consuming media.[3] Even without a court order, we willingly don electronic monitoring devices for tracking our precise location, movement, and bodily functions. We crave the adrenaline that comes from breaking news alerts. Like well-trained Pavlovian dogs, we eagerly await the positive affirmation of a little blue thumbs-up or a small pink heart. Our brains produce a surge of dopamine with every ding, beep, and vibration.

Over time, these dopamine surges change our brain chemistry. *Neuroplasticity* is the ability of the brain to change based on life experiences. The notion of "use it or lose it" is true when it comes to the brain: repetitive behaviors strengthen circuits and create habits, driving the compulsive pursuit of more frequent and intense dopamine releases. In the long term, these devices do not bring us pleasure and do not make us happy. Staying plugged in becomes something that we must do to

---

2   PR Newswire, "Americans Check Their Phones 96 Times a Day," November 21, 2019, https://www.prnewswire.com/news-releases/americans-check-their-phones-96-times-a-day-300962643.html.

3   Nielsen, "Time Flies: U.S. Adults Now Spend Nearly Half a Day Interacting with Media," July 31, 2018, https://www.nielsen.com/us/en/insights/news/2018/time-flies-us-adults-now-spend-nearly-half-a-day-interacting-with-media.html.

avoid the pain of dopamine's absence and the withdrawal that follows. Once we become addicted to checking the headlines, looking at our phones, or scrolling through social media, each new dopamine surge feeds these urges and causes them to increase with greater demand.

As a psychiatrist and a pastor, we have observed countless examples of unhealthy, out-of-balance, and idolatrous worship of technology. As practitioners—one specializing in mental health, the other specializing in spiritual health—we are concerned about the powerful influence that modern technology has on individuals, families, communities, and society as a whole.

We have witnessed the pain of technology addiction. We know the struggles of unhealthy technology use. For us, this is more than statistics. For us, this is personal.

Dr. Smith has treated children on the brink of suicide, influenced by media that romanticize self-harm and websites detailing how to take one's life. He has gotten truant children back into school after they had become vampires with reversed sleep-wake cycles, up all night playing electronic games and sleeping all day. He has corrected the cognitive distortions of patients convinced that something is wrong with their bodies because of the distorted images of beauty prevalent on the internet. As a psychiatrist, Dr. Smith has witnessed the pernicious power that technology can have over mental health.

Pastor Sutton has provided pastoral care to individuals whose lives have been destroyed by technology. He has visited young adults staying at inpatient psychiatric care facilities because of social media and cyberbullying. He has counseled individuals rocked by the public shame of internet call-out culture. He has worked with couples torn apart by pornography and extramarital text messaging. He has helped people discern the differences between the kingdom of God and the kingdom of Facebook. As a pastor, Trevor has witnessed the pernicious power that technology can have over the soul.

Together, we cover mind, body, and soul. Rather than addressing technology from a narrow viewpoint, we seek to address the ways that technology influences the whole person. This book touches on both mental and spiritual health. It explores technology use through multiple lenses, both psychological and theological, medical and spiritual. The pages that follow contain much-needed correctives and practical wisdom for using technology in healthy and purposeful ways.

God's peace and mercy in Christ Jesus, according to 1 Thessalonians 5:23, impacts the whole person: "Now may the God of peace Himself sanctify you completely, and may *your whole spirit and soul and body* be kept blameless at the coming of our Lord Jesus Christ" (emphasis added). Dealing with only one aspect of the whole person—only the body or only the soul—is an artificial division. Therefore, we must consider how technology negatively and positively impacts the whole person—the spirit, soul, and body.

CITIZENS OF A BRAVE NEW WORLD

Perhaps you think this book is not for you. Perhaps you are reading this and you have never been admitted to an inpatient care facility because of internet shaming. Perhaps you don't struggle with excessive dependence on technology.

Maybe you are a modern-day unicorn: no social media accounts, no internet-connected devices, no smartphone. Maybe you are a pocket watch or flip-phone-clipped-to-your-belt kind of person. Maybe you think that you are not addicted to technology and have a completely healthy relationship with it.

Well, you are wrong.

Technology affects us all. We are all citizens of a brave new world. No one is impervious to the influences of technology and nonstop media stimulation. Even if you are a Luddite, technology is still influencing your mental, physical, and spiritual health. Not only is modern technology profoundly shaping the world, but it is also rapidly altering bodies and souls—transforming brains, relationships, religion, communication, families, and communities. Like the proverbial frog in the pot, we are marinating in a digital media environment, largely unaware of the temperature rising around us until we are boiled. Like it or not, we are all in the pot together.

Again, the story of Lemuel Gulliver can help us understand this point. While voyaging on the sea, Gulliver was shipwrecked and washed ashore. He was unconscious and entirely unaware for a period of time. When he finally awoke, Gulliver found that he had unwillingly become a prisoner:

> I attempted to rise, but was not able to stir: for as
> I happened to lie on my back, I found my arms
> and legs were strongly fastened on each side to the
> ground; . . . I likewise felt several slender ligatures
> across my body, from my arm-pits to my thighs.[4]

Slender ligatures, nearly invisible shackles, held him to the ground. Just one of these gossamer strings would not be strong enough to hold him down. Two of these restraints would impede him for just a moment. However, hundreds and thousands

---

4   Jonathan Swift, *Gulliver's Travels*, ed. Thomas M. Balliet (Boston: D. C. Heath and Co, 1900), part 1, chapter 1, Project Gutenberg, November 26, 2005, http://www.gutenberg .org/files/17157/17157-h/17157-h.htm.

FIGURE 3. Gulliver is tied down by the Lilliputians. Image from Jonathan Swift, *Gulliver's Travels*, ed. Thomas M. Balliet (Boston: D. C. Heath and Co., 1900), Project Gutenberg, November 26, 2005, http://www.gutenberg.org/files/17157/17157 -h/17157-h.htm.

of these cords turned him into a prisoner. He had far greater strength and power than the tiny Lilliputians; nevertheless, the sheer quantity of restraints turned this man-mountain into a marionette.

Technology works in a similar way. One single piece of technology may not be able to enslave us. We can overpower the influence of a single smartphone. We can exert human agency

17

over a news app or Twitter. We can throw off the shackles of email or text messages. Yet the more pieces of technology we have, the harder it is to be free. Every breaking news notification and alert adds an additional shackle.

Liberty languishes with each new gadget. Freedom fades with every new internet-connected device. A web of enslavement ensues. Technology overtakes us.

Like the invisible cords that turned Gulliver into a prisoner, the gossamer fetters of modern technology ensnare us. Modern technology constrains us in unseen ways. Since today's technology is largely wireless, we presume that we are free. Yet when we try to cut the cords, we find that we cannot.

How is it possible to be enslaved unknowingly to modern technology? Several factors contribute to this furtive bondage.

Made Invisible

Seamless integration is one of the primary goals for designers of technology. Many devices are designed to be neither seen nor heard. René Leriche, an influential twentieth-century French surgeon, described health as the silence of the organs. When one's organs are working properly, then those organs are working silently. Appendicitis causes this otherwise silent organ to scream with pain. A stomachache breaks the silence of a properly functioning stomach. Similarly, technology is designed to integrate silently into the daily life of users. Only in its malfunction do we become aware of the technology.

Nobody thinks about an internet router until it stops working. Email servers go unnoticed until a malfunction breaks their otherwise silent operation. Furnaces are made to be neither seen nor heard. Because technology is made to be invisible, it is often difficult for us to become aware of its presence and influence on our lives. When it ceases to work properly, that is the moment we become aware of it.

For example, Trevor was teaching a Bible class on the Book of Isaiah. While talking about the invading Assyrians, someone's iPhone responded by saying, "Sorry, I missed that. Could you say it again please?" Apparently, *Assyria* and *Siri* sounded similar enough to activate the virtual assistant function on the person's phone. The iPhone had been silently listening the entire time; however, it was only in this humorous malfunction that everyone became aware of its presence.

Multiplied Exponentially

Technology is largely seamless, silent, and invisible. Thus, its influence can be multiplied exponentially without us knowing it. If we check our phones an average of 100 times per day, that becomes 36,500 times per year or 365,000 times in a decade. If we consume an average of 11 hours of media per day, that becomes 4,015 hours per year. Put another way, that comes out to 167 full days of media consumption each year.

While the individual interactions are barely perceptible in the moment, the aggregate is astounding: How many glances from your child or spouse do you miss in a lifetime of scrolling through news alerts and Facebook? How many thoughts are left unopened while binge-watching shows every night for a decade? How many conversations are never had because headphones plug our ears whenever we go out in public? How many moments are forever lost when we reach for our phones to take a picture every time something memorable happens? Multiplied over a lifetime, the aggregate numbers are disturbing.

Modified Slowly

Since technology use is invisible and accumulating, it

modifies users very slowly. Nobody uses social media once and immediately becomes an envious, judgmental, anxious mess. Installing a news app with notifications does not instantly turn you into a distracted insomniac in need of psychiatric care. Purchasing a streaming subscription will not suddenly diminish the amount of time you spend in Bible reading or prayer. This all happens slowly and methodically. In fact, it happens so slowly that it can only be noticed over a long period of time.

Marshall McLuhan, an influential twentieth-century media theorist, suggested in his book *Understanding Media: The Extensions of Man* that technology has the power to modify users so that they become like the technology they are using. In other words, users conform to what they use. This sentiment echoes the words of Psalm 115:

> Their idols are silver and gold, the work of human hands. They have mouths, but do not speak; eyes, but do not see. They have ears, but do not hear; noses, but do not smell. They have hands, but do not feel; feet, but do not walk; and they do not make a sound in their throat. *Those who make them become like them; so do all who trust in them.* (verses 4–8, emphasis added)

By constantly embracing technologies, we slowly become like these technologies. Nicholas Carr, in his book *The Shallows: What the Internet Is Doing to Our Brains*, argues that using the internet has profound neurological effects; the hypertext environment of the internet modifies the brain to prefer consuming information in a hypertext arrangement. This insight can be extended to other forms of modern technology: as news apps steadily provide instantaneous pellets of information, users come to crave and depend on this sort of immediate feedback. Brilliant colors on digital devices alter how we experience color in nondigital realms.

At a patient and plodding pace, technology modifies us slowly yet profoundly.

REDEEMING TECHNOLOGY

Our excessive technology use comes with a cost. Technology is distracting and not the time-saver it is promised to be; although we may try to multitask, our brains are not built for this level of distraction. The fallout from these distractions ranges from taking twice as long to finish work projects to dying in a car crash from texting while driving. Increased screen time is also costing us our health: poor physical and mental health, excessive weight gain linked to sedentary lifestyles, and increased rates of depression, anxiety, and suicide are all associated with excessive technology use. Worshiping technology requires us to sacrifice more than just our focus and well-being. Spending our lives staring at screens also means sacrificing face-to-face conversations, physical contact, exercise, family time, spiritual practices, and sleep.

It is obvious that devotion to technology comes at a cost. What is less obvious is this: enslavement has the hope of freedom. If someone is taken hostage, that same person can also be set free. If someone has become a captive, he or she may hope in the prospect of redemption.

The word *redeem* has entered the English language by way of Latin. It means "to buy back, take back, or gain again." Redemption is an important theme in the Scriptures. God promises to redeem Israel from their captivity in Egypt: "Say therefore to the people of Israel, 'I am the LORD, and I will bring you out from under the burdens of the Egyptians, and I will deliver you from slavery to them, and I will redeem you with an outstretched arm and with great acts of judgment'" (Exodus 6:6). In the New Testament, Jesus is revealed as the divine Redeemer from sin, death, and the devil (Luke 24:21; Galatians 3:13; Titus 2:14; Hebrews 9:15). Elsewhere in Scripture, God's Word depicts what it looks like to live as released and redeemed people (Galatians 5:1; 2 Corinthians 3:17; 1 Peter 2:16).

The grace of God in Christ Jesus and the Word of God in Scripture, along with the insights of medical practitioners and scholarly research, can redeem technology. Modern technology can be—and must be—redeemed. We have hope even in captivity!

Redeeming technology means reclaiming a right relationship with it. Redeeming technology is establishing healthier habits of technology use and media consumption. Redeeming technology is using it with purpose to glorify God and to serve our neighbor.

The key to redeeming technology is having the right center of gravity. If the wrong object or person is at the center of your universe, then everything else is unbalanced. If the center is not capable of holding all things together, then it will all fall apart.

History has proven this point. Take the solar system, for example. In the ancient world, a popular model placed the Earth as the center of gravity, while the sun, moon, planets, and stars revolved around it. But in order for this model to function, it had to be incredibly complex and convoluted. Over time, this model became less and less accurate, leading sixteenth-century scientists to assert that the wrong object had been placed at the center of the system. The sun, rather than the Earth, was the proper center. Shifting the center of gravity altered the entire system, and it made everything much clearer and simpler.

Likewise, we're in for disaster if technology is at the center of our lives. Our mental, physical, and spiritual health become unbalanced. Technology is not capable of holding all things together. Fitbits, iPhones, and laptops do not have what it takes to be God.

However, Jesus is capable of holding all things together: "And He is before all things, and in Him all things hold together" (Colossians 1:17). Since God commanded us to have no other gods before Him (Exodus 20:3), the god of technology must be dethroned from the center of our lives. God, not technology, is the rightful center of all things.

Redeeming technology begins by having the true Redeemer—Jesus Christ—at the center of our lives. The rest of this book will unpack this concept and explore what this looks like in daily life by employing much-needed correctives and healthier patterns of technology use.

CONCLUSION

While the authors come from different perspectives, psychiatric and pastoral, they are witnessing the same phenomena. We believe that our mental health is intricately interwoven with our spiritual health. Digital media impact us all, often in a negative fashion, both mentally and spiritually.

Nevertheless, modern technology is not beyond redemption. We can have hope. It can be used well. It can be used for good. It can be used purposefully and in ways that do not diminish our well-being. It can be used for the glory of God. Redeeming technology is possible. And it begins in Jesus Christ.

DISCUSSION QUESTIONS

1. What have been some of the biggest technological advancements of the past ten years?

2. Which technological advancement has had the biggest impact on your life? What positive and negative impacts has it had on you?

3. How do you believe technological advancements have impacted those around you? How have they impacted the world?

4. What are your worries for the future with our current technology and possible future advancements?

DO THIS, NOT THAT

AUDIT, COUNT, AND EVALUATE

The Book of Numbers may seem like a tedious read. (Unless, of course, you are an accountant. Then it is an exhilarating, nonstop thrill ride of numbers.)

It may strike us as odd when we come across a Bible verse that merely reports the number of people who have been counted: "The people of Reuben, Israel's firstborn, their generations, by their clans, by their fathers' houses, according to the number of names, head by head, every male from twenty years old and upward, all who were able to go to war: those listed of the tribe of Reuben were 46,500" (Numbers 1:20–21). Why does that even matter? And why is that divinely inspired Scripture? Doesn't the Holy Spirit have better things to do than oversee an audit of the tribes of Israel?

Unlike David's audit of the people in 2 Samuel 24, this one was divinely appointed: "The LORD spoke to Moses in the wilderness of Sinai, in the tent of meeting, on the first day of the second month, in the second year after they had come out of the land of Egypt, saying, 'Take a census of all the congregation of the people of Israel, by clans'" (Numbers 1:1–2). God deemed it necessary to have an accurate count of the people of Israel so there could be order within the camp. Having a precise numbering of the people allowed for an organized journey through the wilderness and preparation to enter the Promised Land.

The point is this: Details matter. Numbers are important. Measuring leads to managing.

This is true when it comes to people and tribes. It's true when it comes to technology too. In order to establish healthier patterns of technology use, it is helpful to do an ACE (Audit, Count, Evaluate).

Audit. Try not to fall out of your chair with excitement when you read this word. Few words inspire boredom and ennui like the word *audit*. Nevertheless, this will not be as painful as you might think. Performing a technology audit can be relatively painless, and it will provide a great foundation for developing a purposeful relationship with technology. While a technology audit can take several different shapes and be tailored to your own situation, the key is writing it down. Do not just put this together in your head. Instead, grab a piece of paper and a pen or some other way to record your audit. The goal of this technology audit is to conduct a review of your technology use on a daily, weekly, or monthly basis.

Count. Essentially, a technology audit entails a lot of counting. Consider the following: How many devices do you regularly use? How many electronic devices are in your household? How many internet-connected devices do you own? Which ones do you spend the most time using? How much time do you spend using each of them? Which social media sites do you frequent most often? What is your total daily screen time? You can use a stopwatch along with a pencil and paper for this exercise. Also, note that some devices perform this function for you by monitoring total screen time and measuring which apps you use the most. Feel free to count whatever you think would be most helpful to you and your own technology use.

Evaluate. Finally, a technology audit not only counts but also evaluates. This means looking not only at the time and numbers but also at the impact that technology use has on you, your relationships, and your well-being. Consider the following: How does your use of technology make you feel? Which devices do you feel like you cannot live without? Do you walk away from using a particular device or platform feeling better or worse? Do something really crazy and ask your spouse, children, or parents what they think about your technology use. Do they think it detracts from your relationship with them or contributes to it?

The point of this ACE is to establish a baseline for your technology use. As you read this book, the insights gained from this exercise will help you to have a clearer picture of how technology intersects with your daily habits and interactions with others.

CHAPTER 2

UNDERSTANDING TECHNOLOGY

A craftsman named Bezalel hammered, hewed, and carved with adroit fingers and an astute mind. Filled with the Spirit of God, Bezalel could mold gold, cut stone, carve wood, and create better than just about anyone. Living in the ancient Near East around the 1400s BC, this man was a wealth of technological ability, intelligence, knowledge, and craftsmanship.

A city planner named Robert measured, marked, and drew up plans for a new parkway. Filled with suspicion about the sort of people who use public transit, Robert made sure that the bridges on this new parkway were just low enough that city buses could not get through. Living in New York City in the 1930s, this man was a powerful authority on the construction of roads, bridges, and public infrastructure.

A middle school student raised her hand during Bible class. Filled with fear about reading in front of a group, she went ahead anyway and offered to read the Bible verse aloud. But just as she found the proper place on her Bible app, the battery on the digital tablet died. So she blurted out the first thing that came to her mind: "My Bible died!"

A throng of people packed the streets of Nottingham, England. Filled with the courage of their leader, Ned Ludd, they marched to a nearby textile factory. Hammers in hand, they forcefully broke into the building and bludgeoned a power loom to its untimely death. Living in the early Industrial Revolution in Europe, these individuals made it their mission to murder machines.

DIFFERENT STORIES, SAME SUBJECT

These stories have nearly nothing in common. They occurred in radically different times: fifteenth century BC, twentieth century AD, present day, and nineteenth century AD. These stories had radically different settings: the ancient Near East, New York, a church classroom, and a factory. And these stories deal with a disparate range of events such as skillful craftsmanship, nefarious civil engineering, Bible study, and industrial revolt. It would seem that these stories have little—perhaps nothing—in common.

Except for technology.

Each of these stories illustrates something about technology that will be explained throughout this chapter. Whether it is hammering gold for the tabernacle or hammering power looms in violent revolt, these different stories all deal with the same subject. And they begin to demonstrate how truly massive the topic of technology can be.

When we think of technology, we may think of modern gadgetry and new inventions such as electric cars, virtual reality, artificial intelligence, and supercomputers. These new technologies come to mind because they are most apparent in society; their newness causes them to be conspicuous and obvious. However, technology is far more than just new gadgetry and recent developments. Technology includes things that are ancient and mundane, physical and nonphysical. Technology includes language and paper clips, bridges and bombs, stone tablets and digital tablets.

Before we can understand technology and use it with purpose, we need to see it for what it is. Before we can see technology for what it is, we need to speak about it with clarity and truth. To that end, this chapter will provide a biblical and scholarly overview of technology as a foundation for the rest of the book.

SCRIPTURE AND TECHNOLOGY: THE LANGUAGE OF CREATION

When Jesus is at the center of our lives, we will increasingly think and talk like Him. It's pretty simple, really: students sound like their teacher and children resemble their parents. Jesus said, "It is enough for the disciple to be like his teacher, and the servant like his master" (Matthew 10:25). The disciples of Jesus speak like He does. The children of God listen to the Father's Word.

Before we can use technology like Christians, we must talk about technology like Christians.

Scripture gives us the proper language and narrative for redeeming technology. Rather than relying on the world's words and knowledge about technology, the followers of Jesus use the language of creation—*Creator, creation, creature,* and *creativity*—to speak about technology. By using the language and narrative of Scripture, we can foster a peculiarly Christian use of technology. This does not mean that we cannot use the word *technology* to talk about these things. But it does mean that we also rely on a rich biblical understanding to help us see and speak about what the world calls technology.

Creation and Goodness

In the beginning, the biblical narrative depicts how goodness is native to God's creation. The common refrain throughout

Genesis 1—"And God saw that it was good"—does not allow us simply to dismiss creation as evil or inherently bad. As if the steady affirmation of goodness were not enough, God concludes His work of creation with a superlative declaration of goodness: "And God saw everything that He had made, and behold, it was very good" (Genesis 1:31).

Many ancient religions such as Gnosticism, Zoroastrianism, and Greek mythology saw creation as the result of evil or bad intentions. Many modern religious outlooks or worldviews such as nihilism see creation as inherently connected with suffering or meaninglessness. Scripture, however, does not support these views. Goodness is native to God's creation.

Called to Creativity

Human creatures have been charged with the work of embellishing creation with their own creative sweat (Genesis 1:28–30). God charged His human creatures with the task of making new things and living creative lives. This is stunning when you stop and think about it. God has subcontracted the work of creating new life to parents. God has told His creatures to "be fruitful and multiply" (Genesis 1:22, 28). The work of creating and re-creating has been given to God's creation in general and human creatures in particular: "The LORD God took the man and put him in the garden of Eden to work it and keep it" (Genesis 2:15).

Creating things—bricks, buildings, books, babies, and even other things that don't start with the letter *B*—is part of our God-given identity. We are living a fully human life when we are creating new things and contributing to the flourishing of God's creation.

31

Poisoned by Sin

Yet God's Word makes it clear that creation has been poisoned by sin. God's good creation now lives in a liminal state far from its original splendor. Creation and all created things are under the curse of sin: "For the creation was subjected to futility, not willingly, but because of Him who subjected it" (Romans 8:20) That which is created by human creatures and existing in creation—what we often call *technology*—is not what it ought to be. It has been poisoned by sin. And poison, as it is prone to do, leads to death.

Scripture gives us the ability to call a thing what it is. While the world struggles to find the right language to describe things, the followers of Jesus do not. We can confidently say that creation is a good thing gone bad. We can speak with certainty about created things being made and used in the wrong way. We do not have to pretend that all things are good and progressing ever onward and upward. Nor do we need to convince ourselves that everything we make or use is meaningless matter in the abyss of the universe. Rather, we can speak of creation and created things as having been subjected to sin while also holding on to the hope "that the creation itself will be set free from its bondage to corruption and obtain the freedom of the glory of the children of God" (Romans 8:21).

Redeemed by Jesus

Creation has not been abandoned by its Creator. On the contrary, the Creator has come into His creation in the person of Jesus of Nazareth. God's plan to make all things new has been accomplished through the cross and resurrection of Jesus. Love made manifest, Jesus has paid the price to redeem us from sin and death, evil and despair. Not only has this Redeemer come to us and died for us, He actually wants to spend eternity with us. He is a living Redeemer (Job 19:25–26).

It is worth noting that the cross—the hinge of both human history and salvation history—is a form of technology. Crucifixion was a technique that likely originated with the Assyrians and Babylonians and then gained wider use by the Persians in the sixth century BC.[5] This lethal technique made its way to the Roman Empire by way of Alexander the Great and the Phoenicians in the third century BC. As with any created thing, crucifixion involved a variety of different forms and techniques. And of all things, a wooden cross and metal nails became God's redeeming technology. God used a torture technique and a horrific human technology to redeem all of creation.

Bane and Blessing

In this liminal time between the creation of all things and Christ's promised return, human creatures can use their creative efforts for bane or blessing, verve or violence. Scripture is teeming with examples of people making things. Genesis 11 constructs a towering account of misguided creative efforts in the tower of Babel. Exodus 31 chisels Bezalel into our minds as one whom God filled "with the Spirit of God, with ability and intelligence, with knowledge and all craftsmanship, to devise artistic designs, to work in gold, silver, and bronze, in cutting stones for setting, and in carving wood, to work in every craft" (Exodus 31:3–5).

Sometimes God commands human creatures to create something very specific. For example, in Genesis 6 God gives Noah detailed instructions for making the ark. Similarly, in Exodus 26 God gives Moses verbal blueprints for the tabernacle.

---

5   F. P. Retief and L. Cilliers, "The History and Pathology of Crucifixion," *South African Medical Journal* 93, no. 12 (2003): 938–41, https://pubmed.ncbi.nlm.nih.gov/14750495/.

These accounts make clear that God can and does use created things—technology—for human blessing and flourishing. Scripture tells of times when created things move in a good and peaceful direction, when swords are turned into plowshares (Isaiah 2:4). And Scripture tells us of times when created things move toward violence and disruption, when plowshares are turned into swords (Joel 3:10).

Worship the Creator, Not the Creation

As creatures, we can easily confuse creation with the Creator and thereby ask too much of that which is created (Romans 1:25). Scripture consistently warns about idolatry. Anything that we trust, love, or fear more than God is a false god—an idol. This happened in 2 Kings 18, when the Israelites bowed down and worshiped the bronze serpent known as the Nehushtan. But idolatry isn't just ancient people with poles and statues; the sin of idolatry persists today too. Modern idolatry may take the shape of worshiping other people, such as a spouse or celebrity; the contents of our bank accounts; or our own health, success, or pleasure. Any form of idolatry—ancient or modern—involves worshiping created things instead of the Creator. We must always guard against idolatry, repent of our false gods, and receive absolution from the true God.

While certainly not exhausting what God's Word has to say on the matter, this preceding overview is a starting place for using the language and narrative of Scripture as we approach technology. The language of creation—*Creator, creation, creature,* and *creativity*—can help us speak about technology in a clear and biblical way. The narrative of Scripture shows us how human creativity and creations fit into God's greater plan and purposes for creation. With this biblical framework in place, we can join the conversation and consider what the world has to say about technology.

JOINING THE CONVERSATION

The late literary theorist Kenneth Burke is well-known for his "unending conversation" metaphor.[6] Burke likened intellectual discussions to an unending conversation taking place in the parlor of human society. He used this illustration to describe the conversations around certain topics—technology, medicine, beauty, mathematics, or any other topic of scholarly concern—that have been happening through the centuries.

Burke invites us to imagine that people arrive in a room and begin discussing a particular topic. As the conversation gets going, it moves in different directions as new people enter into the conversation. Sometimes it loops back to a previous part of the discussion; sometimes it moves in a radically new direction. You arrive in the room and begin to listen to the conversation, picking up the various threads and hearing from the different speakers. At some point, you may even insert yourself into the conversation and help take it in a new direction. But, alas, the night gets late and you must leave the conversation while it continues on long into the night.

This illustration can help us understand the unending conversation that has been taking place around the topic of technology. These discussions have predated our arrival, and they will continue long after our departure. While we find ourselves at a certain time and place in the conversation, it is invaluable to know something of what others have added to the conversation

---

6   See Kenneth Burke, *The Philosophy of Literary Form* (Berkeley: University of California Press, 1941).

before us. This will help us understand what others think about technology and bring God's Word to bear against these ideas.

What Is Technology?

Technology can be very difficult to reduce to a single definition. Various thinkers have defined and discussed technology in radically different ways. Some scholars define technology in fairly narrow ways, limiting it to physical objects such as machines, computers, and gadgets. Others have argued that technology also includes the nonphysical, such as knowledge. Some thinkers have said that technology can only be held in your hand, while others have said that technology can also be held in your head.

For example, many ancient philosophers described technology as being a craft or a skill. Plato described medicine, farming, painting, and carpentry all as forms of *technê*, the Greek word from which we get our word *technology*. These crafts and skills are practiced by an individual and often result in a created thing, such as a painting or a building. Some modern scholars, such as the twentieth-century French philosopher Jacques Ellul, have understood technology in this broad sense. Ellul argued that technology (*la technique*) should be understood as standardized means for absolute efficiency. In other words, an assembly line is an example of technology because it creates a standardized way of efficient production. The same could be said for a recipe for making bread, since it offers standardized steps to produce a loaf of bread in an efficient manner. In short, techniques are technology.

Other scholars define technology more narrowly. A commonly used definition comes from the sociologist Read Bain, who described technology as tools, machines, utensils, weapons, and other sorts of devices. Bain also includes nonphysical skills and knowledge—techniques—in his definition of technology. However, the main focus is on physical objects. Langdon Winner, an influential contemporary scholar of technology, has used "modern practical artifice" as a definition for technology.[7]

Ultimately, technology is all of the above. It is physical and nonphysical, new creations and ancient artifacts. Technology is a prototype autonomous vehicle or a smartphone. And technology is also the ancient techniques used to combine ingredients in order to make a loaf of bread.

Is Technology Good or Bad?

It is naive to argue that technology is wholly good or bad. A far more nuanced understanding maintains that technology is an incongruous compound of good and bad, helping and harming. This understanding accords with the biblical narrative of sinful creatures using their God-given abilities to create things in the context of a fallen world.

However, nuancing the extent to which technology is either good or bad, healthy or unhealthy, has been a long-standing struggle throughout human history. The Luddites, briefly mentioned at the start of this chapter, arose in the early Industrial Revolution in Europe—a time of intense change due to technological advancements, such as the power loom. While some saw the power loom as a good thing that resulted in cheaper clothing, the Luddites saw these machines as destroying their lives and livelihoods. Some saw the technology of the power loom as good; others saw it as being so bad that it must be destroyed.

Consider these other examples of technology: Antibiotics treat bacterial infections. Antibiotics do not treat viral

---

7 Langdon Winner, "Do Artifacts Have Politics?" in *The Whale and the Reactor*, ed. Langdon Winner (Chicago: University of Chicago Press, 1986), 22.

infections. And overuse of antibiotics—taking them for the wrong purpose, for example—can lead to antibiotic resistance, lowering their effectiveness and resulting in increased morbidity and mortality. Washing your hands thoroughly once reduces the risk of infection. But washing your hands ten times in a row, multiple times a day, day after day, leads to dry, cracked skin and increased risk of infection. Power looms, antibiotics, handwashing—are they good or bad? As you can see, it depends.

It can be helpful to nuance the question itself: Is technology good or bad *for what*? Every technological advancement has unintended and often unforeseen effects. In terms of human health and medicine, there has never been a medication without potential side effects. The key is to minimize the risks and maximize the benefits. The use of technology for technology's sake tends to worsen this risk-to-benefit ratio. Taking a daily dose of aspirin simply for the purpose of taking aspirin comes with risks but really no benefit; of course, this changes if you take it for the purpose of preventing a heart attack. Similarly, taking a daily dose of time on your smartphone just to use your phone comes with risks but really no benefits. Again, this changes if you use your smartphone to contact someone. Answering the question of whether technology is good or bad requires thoroughly knowing what purpose the technology serves.

Another and perhaps more fruitful way to look at this issue is to ask whether technology has a healthy or an unhealthy function in an individual's life. Recognizing the unhealthy effects of technology in one's life is a crucial step toward change. In the transtheoretical model of behavioral change, first developed by psychologists in the late 1970s, a person who is unaware of a problem is several steps away from making a positive life change. In this stage, called precontemplation, the individual tends to defend current unhealthy patterns. However, through increased understanding and recognition of the negative impacts of technology, there can be consideration of change and eventually action.

For someone to receive a psychiatric diagnosis, there needs to be impairment, distress, or both. Most uses of technology can turn into disorders if used inappropriately or in excess. A person can develop an addiction to the internet, video games, or any other sort of technology. Yet many people can use technology without it turning into a disorder. Should everyone avoid technology entirely just because it is possible to develop an addiction to it?

Despite the pitfalls of technology, complete avoidance is not the answer. Many people die every day in motor vehicle accidents. Does that mean you should trade in your car and just walk everywhere or hop on a horse? Many people use computers to fuel their addictions. Does that mean that computers cannot also be used to learn, create, and flourish? The positive aspects of technology reflect the Creator. In some sense, this is what J. R. R. Tolkien described as "sub-creation" in his essay *On Fairy Stories*: people can engage in creative and constructive labor that reflects the goodness of God. While some uses of technology reflect humanity's sinful nature, other uses allow humans to be creative like our Creator—to be more fully human. Take away all technology, and you actually become less human. Therefore, we can critique technology without rejecting it completely.

Is Technology Neutral or Biased?

This question is connected to the previous one. Many people argue that technology is neither good nor bad, that it's entirely neutral and it all depends on what the user does with it. A car can be used to drive to church or to drive into a crowd of people. A hammer can be used to build a house or to bludgeon a helpless person. It's all in how you use the tool or technology. While this view is correct and sometimes helpful, we can deepen our understanding.

The bridges on the Southern State Parkway in Long Island, New York, show how this issue is not as simple as we might think. This twenty-five-mile-long parkway stitches together regional airports, parks, churches, colleges, and neighborhoods on Long Island. Construction of the parkway took place primarily under the direction of Robert Moses from 1925 to 1962. Moses, a prolific city planner and public official in the region, heavily influenced the area through the various projects that he directed. Parks, bridges, and highways are an enduring legacy of Robert Moses and his public work. But this legacy may not be entirely innocuous.

Several scholars[8] have argued that Moses used technology to manipulate society in furtive ways. Many of the bridges and overpasses on the Southern State Parkway were deliberately designed to be too low for buses to use. According to biographers, Moses was overt in his prejudice against minorities and lower-income families. By setting the height of bridges in such a way that public transit could not use the parkway, Moses was able to prevent lower-income residents, including many immigrants and minorities, from accessing the nearby beaches and parks. These forms of public technology—bridges, overpasses, and parkways—served some and segregated the rest.

Ordinary things such as bridges and overpasses can pos-

---

8   See, for example, Robert Caro, *The Power Broker* (New York: Vintage, 1974), and Jennifer Slack and Macgregor Wise, *Culture and Technology: A Primer*, 2nd ed. (New York: Peter Lang, 2014).

sess subtle biases. The technology scholar Langdon Winner argues in his influential article "Do Artifacts Have Politics?" that technology is not simply a neutral tool waiting to be used well or poorly, for good or bad, or something in between. Instead, Winner argues that all tools and technologies have been designed to predispose us toward certain patterns, behaviors, and consequences.

A simple example of this can be seen in how scissors are usually made for right-handed individuals. This tool has been designed in such a way so as to predispose users to operate them with the right hand and not the left hand. Similarly, auditorium seats with folding tablet arms (those small desks that swing out for writing and then tuck away when not in use) are almost always on the right side of the seat, because roughly 90 percent of users are right-handed. These design features predispose users toward certain patterns and behaviors. (Can you tell that one of the authors is left-handed and apparently has an ax to grind?)

This is an admittedly brief treatment of a very complicated matter. However, it is fair to say that technology is not nearly as neutral or unbiased as it might initially appear. Designers, engineers, programmers, and others make important design decisions that influence how objects can or cannot be used. We will explore this topic in greater detail throughout this book.

Is Technology in the Foreground or Background?

The seventeenth-century Dutch artist Clara Peeters is known for her painting *Still Life with Cheeses, Almonds, and Pretzels*. This painting has several items in the foreground: various foods, plates, glasses, and jugs. Yet the painting also contains some hidden objects in the background. Peeters signed her name into the knife handle. Additionally, Peeters painted

41

her own portrait into the serving jug; the pewter jug reveals a hidden reflection of the painter's own face. Both of these features are nearly invisible unless one is consciously looking for them. This one painting contains both objects clearly seen in the foreground as well as some that are hidden in the background.

In many ways, technology can be like this painting. Technology, once it has been thoroughly incorporated into society and daily life, can drift into the background and become largely invisible. Don Ihde, a modern philosopher of technology, has described the various ways in which technology can be in the foreground or background of daily life. In his book *Technology and the Lifeworld*, Ihde identifies several different ways in which technologies can function in relation to humans. *Embodied* technologies, such as glasses and hearing aids, become so intimately tied to users that they become a medium through which the world is experienced. Another way of relating to technologies includes *hermeneutic* relationships, in which a technology is used to read something beyond itself. For example, a thermometer offers a temperature reading. A third way in which humans relate to technology, what Ihde called *alterity*, occurs when the technology is made to be interacted with by the human user. For example, robots or smart speakers are technologies made for direct human interaction.

Ihde also proposes a fourth way in which humans can experience technology: *background* relations. These sorts of technologies dwell in the background of daily life. Rather than being a conscious focal point or medium through which the world is experienced, these technologies become silent fixtures in society. Examples of these sorts of technologies include air conditioners and furnaces; while they are made to be neither seen nor heard, their influence is felt as they subtly transform a particular environment and shape daily life.

Only when it malfunctions do we become aware of certain technologies. Internet routers are invisible until they cease to work properly—only then do you think about this background technology. As mentioned in the introduction to this chapter, digital tablets are taken for granted until they run out of power. One is hardly aware of the technology used for reading the Bible until it runs out of power and someone blurts out, "My Bible died!" Only then does it become strangely obvious that one's Bible could be described as dead.

Whether it is in the foreground or background of daily life, technology exerts an influence on us. Ordinary eyeglasses or augmented reality eyeglasses, air conditioners or AI machine learning, created things are powerful forces in our lives and in our world. We may or may not be conscious of their presence, but this does not detract from the power they have to transform how we live and move and have our being.

Can Technology Save Us or Not?

In his book *Superintelligence: Paths, Dangers, Strategies*, philosopher Nick Bostrom argues that superintelligent machines will one day surpass human beings and become the dominant life-form on earth. Bostrom depicts artificial intelligence and machine learning as godlike forces in the world with ultimate power. If these digital deities are made to be benevolent, then they will have the power to save the world and all humanity. If these digital deities are poorly produced, then they will become digital despots and enslave the whole of humanity. Bostrom argues that it all depends on how humans make these superintelligent computers.

Bostrom, along with many other technologists and philosophers who share his same sentiments, believes that technology can save us. If we just design the right devices, create the correct code, and then get out of the way, salvation will come through technology. Artificial intelligence and computer learning, autonomous vehicles and terraforming other planets, transhumanism and genetic engineering are often described as holding limitless possibilities for destroying death and disease. And yet these same philosophers and technologists also fear the possibility of a misaligned intelligence in which technology goes terribly awry and enslaves humanity while destroying the world. Will technology bring about utopia or utter calamity? No consensus exists among philosophers and technologists.

The Christian faith approaches this question with a unique perspective. On the one hand, the Christian faith confesses that humanly created technology cannot independently save the world. No matter how much technology progresses, it will never vanquish sin, death, and the devil. This task is simply and utterly beyond the reach of humanity. Faster microchips, smarter computers, better techniques—these gains will never fix the fatal sin within us all. Nevertheless, Christians have a unique way of entering into this conversation. In a certain sense, the Christian faith affirms that technology has been used to save the world. God used a peculiar form of technology—the ancient torture device of the Roman cross—to save the world through Christ Jesus. Nails, rope, and wood were bound together with the tools and technologies crafted by people. Metal pierced the skin of Jesus according to the established techniques of crucifixion. Although it was a macabre and horrific technology, God used death on a cross to bring about eternal life and salvation.

Can technology save us? No, not in the way that most people today talk about technology saving the world.

Can technology save us? In a certain sense, yes. God has used the cross of Christ Jesus to save us. God has taken the mundane things of this earth, combined them with His amazing grace, and won life and salvation for us.

CONCLUSION

Christians have a unique perspective on technology. While the followers of Jesus fully engage in the unending conversations—both scholarly and popular—surrounding technology, we also unabashedly think and speak about it in uniquely Christian ways. In this regard, Christians may have a peculiar approach to created things. Rather than uncritically accepting new technologies or looking to these items to save us, Christians freely admit that creatures and their creations have limitations. Similarly, Christians do not merely rely on the world's words and knowledge about technology; instead, the followers of Jesus use the language of creation—*Creator, creation, creature*, and *creativity*—to speak about technology.

In this way, we can begin relating to technology in better, healthier, and more godly ways.

DISCUSSION QUESTIONS

1. How do the various definitions of technology described in this chapter compare with how you typically define technology?

2. Choose one form of digital technology. How is it good or bad? How is it neutral or biased? How does it run in the foreground or background of your life?

3. Think about the problems in your life. What role does technology play in these problems?

4. How might you personally think and speak about technology in uniquely Christian ways? How might your life serve as a witness to the Christian conviction that technology cannot save us?

DO THIS, NOT THAT

EYES TO SEE, EARS TO HEAR

Jesus often taught in parables. Some people found this frustrating or difficult. Others found it engaging and enlightening. The difference, according to Jesus, is a matter of eyes and ears:

> Then the disciples came and said to Him, "Why do You speak to them in parables?" And He answered them, "To you it has been given to know the secrets of the kingdom of heaven, but to them it has not been given. For to the one who has, more will be given, and he will have an abundance, but from the one who has not, even what he has will be taken away. This is why I speak to them in parables, because seeing they do not see, and hearing they do not hear, nor do they understand. Indeed, in their case the prophecy of Isaiah is fulfilled that says: ' "You will indeed hear but never understand, and you will indeed see but never perceive." For this people's heart has grown dull, and with their ears they can barely hear, and their eyes they have closed, lest they should see with their eyes and hear with their ears and understand with their heart and turn, and I would heal them.' But blessed are your eyes, for they see, and your ears, for they hear." (Matthew 13:10–16)

According to Jesus, His followers had eyes and ears that were capable of seeing and hearing. By the power of the Holy Spirit, they were able to perceive what was really being communicated through the parables that Jesus told.

In some sense, technology can be like a parable: it contains more than we readily perceive. Like a parable, technology can be both simple and complex, clear and hidden. Therefore, it is important for us to have eyes that can see and ears that can hear when it comes to our interactions with technology.

Read the Scripture passages below and look for references to technology. Then reflect on how these passages might relate to the use of technology in this world or your own use of technology.

Isaiah 40:18–26

Genesis 6:11–22

2 Timothy 4:13

Psalm 115

As you interact with Scripture, consider other passages that depict technology or created things in some way. It is vital for the people of God to comprehend the world around us on the basis of God's Word. Rather than fixing our eyes on and tuning our ears to worldly understandings of technology, we allow God's Word to be the norm and rule for all things. God's Word is the measure and basis of reality. The definition, value, and purpose of created things—what the world calls technology—is not determined by Apple, Google, or Wikipedia. Rather, God sets the parameters for creation and creatures in the Word. Through the Word of God, the Holy Spirit opens our eyes so that they can truly see and opens our ears so that we can truly hear.

CHAPTER 3

TECHNOLOGY
AND MENTAL HEALTH

A young artist named Werther, sensitive and passionate, suffers from unrequited love for a young woman. Unable to tolerate a broken heart, he takes his own life.

A young high school student suffers mistreatment from others. Unable to tolerate the effects of this trauma, she takes her own life and leaves behind cassettes that blame individuals for her demise.

Two deaths, two hundred years apart. Both of these are fictional deaths that have likely contributed to real-life suicides. *The Sorrows of Young Werther* was produced by way of printing press technology. This book, written by Johann Wolfgang von Goethe, was published in 1774 and reputedly led to the first documented cases of copycat suicide. The other example, *13 Reasons Why*, was produced by way of digital technology for a 2017 Netflix series based on the book by Jay Asher. This popular series was accused of not following media recommendations for responsibly depicting suicide, with some studies suggesting an association between the series and an increase in youth suicide,[9] especially among young females.

---

9   National Institute of Mental Health, "Release of '13 Reasons Why' Associated with Increase in Youth Suicide Rates," April 29, 2019, https://www.nimh.nih.gov/news/science-news /2019/release-of-13-reasons-why-associated-with-increase-in-youth-suicide-rates.shtml.

An old book and a new streaming series. How is it that these two different forms of media, though centuries apart, can influence real people to mimic fictional characters and even take their own lives? Technology and mental health are interrelated. Our mental health is impacted by using devices, staring at screens, streaming shows, reading posts, viewing pictures, and checking notifications.

THE SLOW COOK OF DIGITAL MEDIA

Way beyond books and television shows, the term *technology*, as explained in the previous chapter, can mean many things. This chapter focuses on the power of technology—specifically digital media and social media—as it relates to mental health.

Mental health involves properly functioning thoughts, behaviors, and emotions. Digital media impact all these domains, and all these domains influence one another. Thoughts influence emotions, which in turn influence behaviors, which affect one's overall mental health. Seeing something through digital media can make you think something. Thinking something can make you feel something. Feeling something can make you do something. Before long, thoughts, behaviors, and emotions that previously functioned properly are altered by these digital media.

For example, you see a picture on Facebook posted by a guy you barely knew in college. He is on vacation with his family in Hawaii, and they all look happy. In fact, they look euphoric. Life could not be better. You think, "I can't afford to take my family on vacation in Hawaii." You also think, "Am I missing out on something really awesome?" You feel bad. Then you search for information about Hawaiian vacations and increase your credit card debt when you purchase an expensive trip to Hawaii.

Seeing, thinking, feeling, and acting intermingled together as a result of a single social media post.

Does it always happen this way? Does every travel post cause us to go into resentful credit card debt? No. Not always. However, it can be very revealing to verbalize how our actions, feelings, and thoughts are formed by consuming digital media. Next time you are scrolling through your usual social media platforms, try verbalizing how each post makes you feel. As you look at someone's political posts, you might say, "This makes me angry." Seeing an Instagram post of a perfect family in which every person—even the five-year-old?!—is smiling and has their eyes open at the same time might cause you to say, "This makes me jealous and a little impressed." While you might feel odd verbalizing these feelings, this exercise will reveal much about how social media make you think and feel.

The influence of digital technology is often subtle and even practically unconscious. We are marinating in a digital culture while the water is warming. But we are all holding the smartphones, spending hours online, and bingeing shows, so nothing seems out of the ordinary. Too distracted to notice the gradually increasing temperature, we have a hard time recognizing the dangers until they become disasters. By the time we feel the burn, we scream out, "How did we get here?"

Over the last two decades, digital technology and its presence in our lives has been rapid and pervasive. Most Americans did not have email addresses until the late 1990s. Facebook was created in 2004, and the first iPhone was released in 2007. Now email, social media, and smartphones are like the air that we breathe. Everyone seems to have smartphones, smartwatches, smart televisions, laptops, desktops, e-readers, and streaming services for music, television, and movies. When it comes to digital media, the days are slow and seem like business as usual, but the years are fast. Consider how much has changed over the past decades and how dependent we are on digital technology for many aspects of our normal daily work and social lives, not to mention during exceptional times such as pandemics or disasters. These massive changes can impact our mental health in profound ways.

It used to be hard to get online; now the challenge is unplugging, getting offline. In the past, if someone had an addiction, it was possible to control access to temptations. You could burn all the *Playboy* magazines or dump out all the alcohol. But now it is different: How can we escape our digital world, even if only for a little while? Things happen fast—measured in months and years, not decades—in our current digitally saturated state. The incessant rate of change surrounding digital media makes it hard for mental health research and information to keep pace.

NEGATIVE EFFECTS OF DIGITAL MEDIA

The fast pace of digital media and modern technological developments means that researchers have not had much time to study the effects of digital technology on mental health. However, we have learned a few things.

The good news is that nobody has gone on Instagram and exploded, leaving a black, inky smear on the ground. The danger is not instantaneous, but it is imminent. According to studies,[10] digital media tend to present a fairly small negative impact on the mental health of most users. In other words, the use of

---

10 See, for example, Victoria Rideout, Susannah Fox, and Well Being Trust, "Digital Health Practices, Social Media Use, and Mental Well-Being among Teens and Young Adults in the U.S.," Providence St. Joseph Health Digital Commons 1093 (Summer 2018), https:// digitalcommons.psjhealth.org/publications/1093/; and David A. Scott, Bart Valley, and Brooke A. Simecka, "Mental Health Concerns in the Digital Age," *International Journal of Mental Health and Addiction* 15, no. 3 (June 2017): 604–13, https://doi.org/10.1007 /s11469-016-9684-0.

digital technology poses only minor mental health risks for the majority of individuals.

For digital technology—as with alcohol and other substances and activities with addictive potential—in general, the heavier the use, the greater the negative health effects. Those most at risk for negative effects are heavy users and those who are already vulnerable to negative effects because of preexisting mental illnesses, including depression, anxiety, and suicidality. For those most at risk, the effects of unconstrained digital technology can be extreme, life-changing, and even deadly.

Mirror Neurons

The power of media such as *The Sorrows of Young Werther* and *13 Reasons Why* comes through contagion. Contagion is a form of social influence in which emotions or behaviors spread from one person to another. All it takes is exposure to someone else for behavior or emotional contagion to occur. And these days, through the internet, we are all exposed to everyone. When we turn on our screens, the world rushes at us in a torrent of digital media. While we are aware of the endless flow of digital media content, we may not realize how these media cause us to mirror the behaviors of others.

Suicide contagion is a well-established construct within the field of psychiatry. Suicide contagion is why the average person's suicide is not splashed on the front page of the local paper. Responsible suicide reporting is part of journalistic ethics. Similar to suicide contagion, behavioral contagion is also seen in self-injury such as cutting; eating disorders such as anorexia nervosa; substance use; teen pregnancy; and youth aggression, to name a few areas of influence.

Why would someone copy the actions of another, especially

unhealthy actions? The answer lies in a part of the brain called mirror neurons. These neurons fire not only when you yourself act but also when you observe someone else performing an action, mirroring those actions. Mirror neurons may be an important part of development through childhood, including social learning through imitation and empathy. Sympathy involves feeling pity for someone else's misfortune, whereas empathy involves really feeling what someone else is experiencing. Without mirror neurons, we would likely experience less empathy, and we would have to guess at the inner experiences of others.

In addition to reflecting the actions of others, mirror neurons may also reflect the emotions of others. This leads to emotional contagion. Contagion has an especially strong influence when the individual exposed already strongly identifies with the influencer through perceived similarities or a desire to become like the other. Think about the rise of endorsements and product placements by online influencers.

In hysterical contagion, sometimes called mass hysteria, rapid contagion causes a group of people to demonstrate physical symptoms due to an underlying psychological process. In 2012, twenty patients in the state of New York (nineteen girls from the same school and one parent) demonstrated Tourette-like symptoms thought to have a psychogenic cause—that is, stemming from the mind rather than a physical condition. The jerking, twitching, flailing, and strange noises resolved over time, but the girls who recovered slowest were the ones most involved with social media. Research finds that increased exposure to social media has a small association with increased depression, suicidality, anxiety, feelings of loneliness, self-harm, body image disturbance, and eating disorders. Mental health professionals suspect that behavioral and emotional contagion underlie cases of worsening mental health with heavy exposure to social media.

Contagion and technology is such an important topic that it will be discussed in greater detail in chapter 9.

Insomnia and Obesity

What's the greatest risk associated with consuming violent media, such as violent video games? You might think it would be behavioral contagion. But studies show a surprising lack of evidence for contagion when it comes to violent video games. Some individuals who play violent video games are also aggressive, but researchers are split on whether the use of violent media is a cause or a symptom of aggression (more on this in chapter 4). Violent video games are low on the list of suspected factors contributing to mass shootings, while other forms of technology such as guns are more strongly implicated. However, mental health professionals do recommend that aggressive youth have restricted access to violent video games. While there is not a well-established link between violent gaming and violence toward others, that doesn't mean excessive video gaming is harmless.

The main victims of excessive video games are usually the gamers themselves. Especially in cases of excessive gaming that takes precedence over other life activities, many negative effects impact the gamer's general health.

Take Billy, for example. While Billy is fictitious, aspects of his story are painfully real, and Dr. Smith has worked with many patients like him. This twelve-year-old boy plays video games all the time. Billy does not join his family for dinner. However, due to a combination of poor diet (snacking during the day and raiding the pantry at night) and lack of exercise, he has gained excessive weight and become obese. He does not go to sleep and instead stays up all night and passes out early in the morning. If he agrees to leave the house, he goes to school looking like a zombie. Billy resists brushing his teeth and showering, and his personal hygiene suffers. Billy so badly wants to continue playing video games that instead of getting up to use the bathroom, he soils and wets his pants in order to keep playing. He steals credit card numbers to make purchases for his video games. Most of these games are free or low cost to begin with, but they later influence users to make in-game purchases. Take the video games away from him, and he cannot handle it. He will go berserk, attacking his parents and destroying property. He may even threaten suicide. He will do anything to protect his precious video game time.

This scenario is not as uncommon as you might think. Additional physical consequences include wrist, neck, and elbow pain, weakness and numbness in hands, fatigue, and migraines. In rare cases, these consequences can even be deadly: deaths from cardiac arrest, seizures, blood clots, and suicide.

But video games are not all bad. When used in moderation they can be a social outlet, since many gamers play with other people. They can also provide a place to blow off steam and teach hand-eye coordination. Additional psychological benefits may help those who suffer from mental disorders and give pleasure to the two billion video gamers worldwide.

Dopamine

How is it possible for a smartphone to be addictive? You cannot drink it, smoke it, or inject it into your veins. It is all about the dopamine. Anything that gives us pleasure causes the release of dopamine in a part of our brains called the *nucleus accumbens*. Digital media are engineered to give us consistent, repeated bursts of dopamine.

For example, we post on Facebook, and getting "likes" makes us happy, at least temporarily. Each burst of dopamine causes positive reinforcement, increasing the chances of us performing the same behavior again to get another burst of dopamine. This is an example of operant conditioning—like a rat in a cage repeatedly pressing a lever to get a reward. We also learn (or you might say we are trained by the device) to associate the various beeps and dings on our phone with pleasure. Simply hearing the notification sound means receiving some sort of pleasure in the form of a like, a favorite, or a message. In this regard, we are just like Pavlov's dog as it was trained to salivate over the sound of the bell in anticipation of food. You can't eat a bell, but it can certainly cause you to salivate in expectation of mealtime. The association of the bell with the actual reward— whether food or eagerly anticipated electronic communication—is an example of classical conditioning.

What creates even more compulsive behaviors is having this reward system run on a schedule of intermittent reinforcement. The rewarding bursts of dopamine are not provided on a regularly scheduled basis. Instead, repeated checking, such as refreshing an inbox, only sometimes results in rewards, and these rewards are presented at random intervals. It's like the slot machine that pays off only occasionally and with no consistent pattern. You end up spending hours pulling the arm of that slot machine in pursuit of the reward—or constantly checking your phone for text messages, new emails, social media updates, and notifications.

We crave the dopamine that comes from repeatedly checking

our phones and are afraid to miss it. This explains why many of us are chained to our phones, doggedly checking for updates, messages, and notifications. The average American consumer now checks his or her smartphone more than 60 times a day. Some reports indicate that people check their phones an average of 100 times per day.[11] With repeated exposure, we develop a tolerance to the rewards that we initially receive from digital media. The more we use the technology, the less pleasurable it becomes over time. A few likes on Facebook or a few more followers on Twitter no longer cuts it. We must increase our use and effort to recapture the pleasure originally received. Going without the dopamine we crave makes us feel lousy, so in addition to seeking pleasure, we also use digital media to avoid bad feelings from lack of dopamine.

This is not unlike a person with alcohol dependence who starts with a six-pack of beer and works his or her way up to a fifth of whiskey because the six-pack no longer gives a buzz. What's a quick and easy way to tell if you may have a problem with digital technology use? Ask yourself: What is the first thing that I reach for in the morning when I wake up? People with alcoholism famously have an "eye-opener," reaching for a bottle first thing in the morning, waking up with intense cravings after a period of sleep without those dopamine bursts. The need for an eye-opener strongly suggests that a person has a problem with alcohol. If you consistently reach for your phone first thing in the morning looking for a dopamine rush from that digital eye-opener, you may have an issue.

Another extreme example, although one that many of us have experienced, is the phantom tingle in your pocket. The

---

11   PR Newswire, "Americans Check Their Phones 96 Times a Day," November 21, 2019, https://www.prnewswire.com/news-releases/americans-check-their-phones-96-times-a-day-300962643.html.

sensation in your pocket feels exactly like a vibrating phone. But the pocket is empty. Technically this is a hallucination of the tactile variety (nothing is there at all) or an illusion (something triggered a response, but it was not what you thought it was). An addicted brain views most stimuli as related to the object of desire, so the wind blowing against your empty pants pocket becomes that phantom tingle. Maybe you were just thinking really hard about your phone and missing it. Digital technology obsession results in a one-track mind.

Miguel de Cervantes depicted Don Quixote as addicted to the dream of becoming a knight. Consumed by this object of desire, Quixote hallucinated that windmills were giants waiting to be vanquished by a courageous knight. While this deluded knight tilted at windmills, we are deluded by the tingle of a vibrating phone that is not there. Yet both of these hallucinations are fueled by an intense pining for something that we desire.

Addictions of all stripes involve a chronic pattern of persistent and repetitive actions and thus involve a cycle of behavior. A cycle does not have a clear ending or beginning; it just goes in circles. The addictive behavior causes one to desire the pleasure and tension relief that comes from the release of dopamine. This, in turn, feeds the addiction and compulsive dopamine-seeking behaviors. Nobody would get addicted if there was not some initial function, whether it be pleasure or relief of pain. The positive sensation is short-lived, followed by the desire for more pleasure, rising tension, and sometimes shame.

Angry and Scared

Happiness and pleasure are not the only things that drive us to use digital media. Anger and fear may also motivate us to check our smartphones, read news sites, and scroll through social media. While we ostensibly want to hear good news from the internet, humanity has a sadistic streak that longs to hear some sort of bad news too (assuming the bad news largely involves others and not ourselves, of course). Although they never say it out loud, the large tech companies know that anger and fear drive consumption. If you are angry or scared, you are likely to spend more time on the internet, clicking from item to item on down the rabbit hole. Since tech companies and news outlets aim to increase the amount of time users spend on a platform and the number of clicks on a page, anger and fear is like rocket fuel helping them reach their goals.

Anger and fear motivate us to action. From a mental health standpoint, both of these feelings can have a legitimate purpose. Anger can serve as a motivator for change: if you're angry enough with your poor health, you commit to a fitness plan. Fear is very helpful if a grizzly bear decided to attack your camping tent at night. However, anger and fear have less purpose on the internet. What are you really going to do with much of the information you are exposed to online, assuming it is even true? What do you really need to know, and what is merely a glut of information made possible by digital technology? How does gossip, such as learning about a celebrity's affair, truly affect your life? How important is it to read about a squirrel thousands of miles away from you that has tested positive for the bubonic plague?

Suppose you are angry or fearful about the injustice of the world or the ways in which others are hurting. Unlike celebrity gossip or an unfortunate little squirrel, matters of injustice and human suffering actually matter. However, will reading about it for two more hours on the internet change anything? Are you going to put down the phone and do something about it?

Wallowing in anger and fear does not make you feel any better, but it does keep you online, searching for more. You may receive some pleasure in the release of tension when anger and fear are discharged, but it's not a healthy way to live. And it is exhausting.

The old nightly news, with its limited hours and defined boundaries, has become the never-ending news. While the nightly news often contained bad news and fear-inducing reports during its broadcast, it was limited to an hour. Viewers experienced respite and relief until the next night. However, with the never-ending news cycle, the bad news continues without pause. And often you hear the same exact bad news on repeat. It's like getting kicked in the gut—fear—and punched in the head—anger—multiple times a day. Much of what we read online is bad news, and most of that bad news is not for us. Thankfully the Good News, the Gospel of Jesus Christ, is for us all.

Too Many Tabs Open

Web browsers allow users to have dozens of tabs open at the same time. Smartphones run multiple apps concurrently. Wearable devices allow users to check their heart rate and email at the same time. While these devices may allow us to multitask, our brains may not. Teens spend an average of nine hours a day on electronics, and some reports have set that number even higher. Nielsen, a media research group, has reported that American adults spend an average of eleven hours each day consuming media.[12] These devices and media consumption deprive us of sleep and lead to more sedentary lifestyles and their related health complications. Spending nine to eleven hours per

---

12 Nielsen, "Time Flies: U.S. Adults Now Spend Nearly Half a Day Interacting with Media," July 31, 2018, https://www.nielsen.com/us/en/insights/news/2018/time-flies-us-adults-now-spend-nearly-half-a-day-interacting-with-media.html.

day with electronic devices means that we spend most of our waking hours multitasking in some way.

However, mental health experts have determined that the concept of multitasking, and being good at it, is a lie. Studies have examined how students perform tasks while multitasking compared to being required to do one task at a time and complete that task before moving on to another. In attempts at multitasking, each task takes more time to complete; moreover, multitasking results in more errors. Students often have multiple screens active while studying or attending lectures. Adults in meetings may easily be off task checking email while not listening to the conversation. It seems that no place is sacred. At church, Bible apps are popular, but it is easy to stray from that app over to messaging apps. People may multitask, but it is not productive work. And the consequences of attempting to multitask can be deadly: it is estimated that thousands of people die every year in the United States because of texting while driving.

BENEFITS OF DIGITAL TECHNOLOGY FOR MENTAL HEALTH

We can also see positive uses and effects of digital devices and internet access. Digital technology can erase the barrier of distance between people. This is especially valuable when people are physically separated due to health concerns, transportation barriers, or other issues that keep them apart. Telehealth, for example, provides medical care to patients who otherwise might not be able to see a doctor. Digital technology can also provide social support through video calls that connect otherwise isolated people. This type of social support can be important for individuals in minority groups where in-person social support in their locales may not always be readily available.

The internet can be a powerful source of mental health information, although it is important to remember that not all of it is accurate. Additionally, mental health apps may provide psychological benefits to patients as an adjunct, and sometimes even a substitute, to in-person care with a mental health provider. Some social media platforms, such as Facebook, have even developed tools to identify users at risk of self-harm and provide help resources. Digital technology is not entirely bad for mental health. The key is to eat the meat but spit out the bones. When using digital technology to benefit our mental health, we must work to avoid consuming many of the harmful elements that come with it.

CONCLUSION

Digital technology does not satisfy in any meaningful, longer-term way. It is largely junk thrown down the bottomless well within us that only God can fully satisfy. As Augustine wrote in his *Confessions*, "Lord, You have made us for Yourself, and our heart is restless until it rests in You."[13] Although he lived in a time before digital technology when only birds tweeted, Augustine knew that restless hearts can only be cured by God. Repeating unhealthy behaviors does not lead to a positive outcome. From a mental health standpoint, restless hearts and minds can be eased by developing coping skills that do not involve digital technology. Restless hearts and minds can find true and eternal rest, peace, fulfillment, and satisfaction only in God.

Turning to digital devices to cure our deep-set guilt and fear, loneliness and frustration, sin and death is like taking

---

13   Adapted from Augustine, *The Confessions of Saint Augustine*, trans. E. B. Pusey, book 1, chapter 1, Project Gutenberg, June 2002, https://www.gutenberg.org/files/3296/3296-h /3296-h.htm.

vitamin C to cure pancreatic cancer. It simply will not work. Just as any good medical practitioner knows both the capabilities and the limitations of a medication, it is vital to keep created things in their rightful place. These creations wrought by human hands and minds can offer a finite amount of pleasure and social connectedness, access to information and assistance in accomplishing tasks. The key word here is *finite*. Only the infinite—only God the Father through God the Son by the power of God the Holy Spirit—can cure all our guilt, fear, loneliness, frustration, sin, and death.

DISCUSSION QUESTIONS

1. How does digital technology influence your mental state in healthy and unhealthy ways?

2. How much time do you spend attending to digital technology each day? How balanced is your time commitment to digital technology versus other life activities?

3. Do you think your use of digital technology is problematic? How would you know if you had a problem? How would you know if this problem became an addiction?

4. How difficult would it be for you to have a digital detoxification and go without digital technology for a while? What would make this challenging? How could you overcome these challenges?

DO THIS, NOT THAT

CULTIVATE MENTAL HEALTH

The Church in Corinth was not well. Their spiritual health suffered as a result of division, disorder, and idolatry. The spiritual illnesses plaguing the individual members contributed to a diminished vitality within the whole community. This prompted the apostle Paul to discuss the ways in which the parts of the body are interconnected:

> For the body does not consist of one member but of many. If the foot should say, "Because I am not a hand, I do not belong to the body," that would not make it any less a part of the body. And if the ear should say, "Because I am not an eye, I do not belong to the body," that would not make it any less a part of the body. If the whole body were an eye, where would be the sense of hearing? If the whole body were an ear, where would be the sense of smell? But as it is, God arranged the members in the body, each one of them, as He chose. If all were a single member, where would the body be? As it is, there are many parts, yet one body. (1 Corinthians 12:14–20)

These verses are part of a larger discourse on the Church as the Body of Christ, but it is also important to notice the basis of Paul's analogy: the human body depends on the harmony of its many members. Mental health is connected to overall bodily health because the brain is connected to the rest of the body. Fostering one aspect of your health and well-being affects other aspects of your health and well-being.

This chapter explored the intersection between technology and mental health. As a way to incorporate this discussion into your own life, consider one of the following actions to foster improved mental health in your life or the life of another.

Healthy habits. Some very basic healthy habits can go a long way to improve mental health. Researchers have found that developing a habit of consistent exercise can benefit mental health. Although people often engage in exercise as a way to promote heart health or maintain a healthy body weight, it is well documented that exercise is good for mental health as well. Similarly, nutrition and mental health are not disconnected; maintaining a well-balanced diet and proper fluids can foster improved mental well-being. Another very basic healthy habit is engaging in meaningful conversation with other people. Establishing a routine of intentional time to converse with another person and invest in a relationship is vital to maintaining mental health. God made this clear from the beginning when He declared, "It is not good that the man should be alone" (Genesis 2:18).

Get help when needed. Talk to someone about mental health questions or concerns you may have. If you were concerned about an arrhythmia with your heart, you would not hesitate to see your primary care physician for fear that she would judge you or think less of you. A physician would not say, "What a freak! You've got an irregular heartbeat!" The same is true when it comes to mental health. A psychiatrist, counselor, or pastor will not think less of you for having mental health concerns. In fact, they chose these professions out of a desire to serve and help people in these very situations. Get help if you have mental health questions or concerns.

Learn more. Educate yourself about mental health through evidence-based online resources (such as the *Facts for Families* series available for free on the American Academy of Child and Adolescent Psychiatry website). Rather than reading some clickbait listicle that you find online, search out information that is peer-reviewed and reputable. Join an advocacy organization online, such as National Alliance on Mental Illness (NAMI). One of the benefits of modern technology is the incredible access that it provides to timely resources.

The human body was made by God to be a harmonious union of many members. Take care of the whole body—the many parts that make up one body—that God has given to you.

CHAPTER 4

RESHAPING
MINDS AND SOULS

"God saw everything that He had made, and behold, it was very good" (Genesis 1:31).

Suppose that God had made a different declaration in the sight of His newly completed creation. Imagine if God beheld His work and said, "This is bad. I have erred greatly in creating this world."

It is troubling when creators denounce their creations. And yet it happens.

Ethan Zuckerman regrets inventing the pop-up ad. In an attempt to distinguish advertisements from websites, Zuckerman devised a way to have advertisements automatically pop-up upon arrival at a particular website. The annoying overuse of this feature has led Zuckerman to regret what he invented.

Vincent Connare, creator of the font Comic Sans, has described his creation as "the best joke I ever told."[14] Having his name forever associated with the Comic Sans font has caused Connare to be both amused and mortified.

Scott Fahlman is credited as creating the first smiley face emoticon (the precursor of emojis) in 1982. As part of an online message board, Fahlman proposed :-) as an easy way to indicate

---

14   Vincent Connare, Twitter post, February 8, 2010, 6:20 a.m., https://twitter.com/Vincent Connare/status/8806817764?s=20.

a joke and :-(as an indication that the post was serious. Since its inception, however, Fahlman has seen the ways that his creation has degraded written communication rather than improve it.

It comes as no surprise that the creators of pop-up ads, Comic Sans, and emoticons/emojis would have some regrets. However, it appears that technology creators *often* regret their work and denounce their creations.

The first president of Facebook, Sean Parker, has publicly lamented his work in helping to create the popular social media platform. Parker stated that "God only knows what [Facebook is] doing to our children's brains."[15] Echoing Parker's sentiments is Chamath Palihapitiya, another former Facebook executive. Palihapitiya has suggested that social media platforms are destroying how society works.[16] Tim Cook, Apple's CEO, has publicly expressed that he does not want his young nephew to use social networks.

A theme is emerging: unlike God, many Silicon Valley technologists behold their various digital creations and are moved to declare, "This is bad. We have erred greatly in creating this technology."

TECHNOLOGY:
PUT OUT, THEN THOUGHT OUT

In his book *Understanding Media*, Marshall McLuhan argues that technology is often put out long before it has been thought out. By this statement, McLuhan does not mean that technology companies fail to test their products thoroughly and

---

15   Mike Allen, "Sean Parker unloads on Facebook: 'God only knows what it's doing to our children's brains,'" Axios, November 9, 2017, https://www.axios.com/sean-parker-unloads-on-facebook-god-only-knows-what-its-doing-to-our-childrens-brains-1513306792-f855e7b4-4e99-4d60-8d51-2775559c2671.html.

16   Julia Carrie Wong, "Former Facebook Executive: Social Media Is Ripping Society Apart," *The Guardian*, December 12, 2017, https://www.theguardian.com/technology/2017/dec/11/facebook-former-executive-ripping-society-apart.

work out all the bugs. In fact, companies invest tremendous time and money into researching and testing their creations. Rather, McLuhan's point is that technology is often hastily put out and used by people before the impact of the technology is thoroughly explored and understood. The technology itself is well thought out, at least at a superficial level, but the ways in which technology impacts users and has the power to reshape minds, souls, and society—the deeper level—is scarcely considered before it is released.

Smartphones, social media platforms, wearable devices, and other creations are handed to us so that we can be the test subjects. Digital devices and apps are brought to market prior to any longitudinal studies on how they might alter our lives, minds, and experiences. Technology is often released, then researched. It is a live ammo exercise. It is like having test subjects ride on a plane high up in the air as it is being built.

Social media platforms go live, users sign up in droves and consume content on a daily basis, and then researchers study how it is transforming our brains and relationships. Video games undergo rigorous usability testing prior to release, but seldom is research done prior to release into how the video game will alter the lives of those who use it on a daily basis. The technology itself is well known, but the side effects of the technology are discovered as we use it. And this all helps explain the frequent regret that technologists have when it comes to many of their creations.

This is a peculiar way of doing things.

By way of comparison, medication and vaccines are heavily researched and go through quality-control processes before they are released. The Food and Drug Administration of the United States regulates all drugs, whether prescription or nonprescription. Clinical trials are performed under well-controlled conditions on volunteers. Once approved, these drugs are carefully manufactured and packaged with accurate and complete information on dose, route, and schedule. This package information also includes safety information regarding known side effects, unsafe drug interactions, contraindications for use (special individual circumstances under which it is too risky to take the drug), and established uses for the drug (conditions it treats effectively).

Additionally, people often do their own sort of research—vetting the information and examining the studies—before taking a medicine or receiving a vaccine. You cannot effectively do your own research without reliable facts at your disposal from evidence-based research. Even with careful research and regulated approval, manufacturing, and packaging processes, the true effectiveness and potential side effects of a medication or vaccine may not be discovered until after it has been released out into the world for weeks, months, or years and tried by millions of people.

Technology production is more akin to the production of dietary supplements, which are treated more like special foods. Prescription drug production is done carefully, with the assumption that drugs are considered dangerous until proven safe. However, dietary supplements are considered safe until proven dangerous. Dietary supplements are often manufactured and released without any clinical trials and without the same standards for manufacturing and packaging processes. This practice has resulted in products tainted with pesticides, germs, and heavy metals. Supplements might contain more or less than the amount of product listed on the label or not contain what is on the label at all. There may even be drugs in the supplements.

As with technology, dietary supplements tend to be self-prescribed. The user usually lacks guidance from a physician and does not benefit from a system for monitoring and reporting side effects. Physicians take an oath to benefit their patients and do no harm. Companies take an oath to profit shareholders; the primary motivation is not necessarily the greater good. Exaggerating claims of effectiveness and minimizing reports of risks both lead to increased profits, and it can be difficult to gauge the truthfulness of claims behind dietary supplements. Tainted by motivation for profit, reviews of dietary supplements are often biased.

Why is there so great a difference between technology (released, then researched) and medicine (researched, then released)? Unlike medication or vaccines, and even dietary supplements, people often do not understand that technology has the power to alter minds, bodies, and souls in meaningful ways. We are convinced that medications have the power to change the physiological workings of our bodies, so we carefully research their impact before using them. On the other hand, we do not understand that digital tablets have the power to reconfigure our minds, souls, behaviors, or beliefs, so we imbibe them without a second thought.

This way of doing things could be disastrous for both individuals and society.

A BIBLICAL CASE STUDY: THE NEHUSHTAN

Scripture offers many examples—both positive and negative—of how created things have the power to alter our minds and souls, behaviors and beliefs. Nehemiah led the project of reconstructing the walls of Jerusalem, which became a powerful catalyst for Israel's renewed identity following captivity. Conversely, Aaron led the effort to fashion gold jewelry into a golden calf so that Israel could worship it as their god. Other biblical examples of the influence of created things include the ark of the covenant, the Nehushtan during the time of Hezekiah, and the apostle Paul's usage of books and parchments (2 Timothy 4:13).

Let's look closely at just one of these examples: the Nehushtan. The Book of Numbers tells of the wilderness sojourn of the Israelites. While in the wilderness, the Israelites were attacked by snakes, and many people died from snakebites. The people asked Moses to pray to God for relief. He prayed, and God told him to make a bronze serpent: "Make a fiery serpent and set it on a pole, and everyone who is bitten, when he sees it, shall live" (Numbers 21:8). This created thing—an assemblage of wood and metal—was initially a great benefit to the people.

It did not take long, however, for this good thing to go bad. The Book of 2 Kings recounts how the people of Israel made offerings to the bronze serpent that Moses had made earlier, which was called Nehushtan (2 Kings 18:4). Although it was initially commissioned by God, this created thing altered the minds, souls, behaviors, and beliefs of God's people. They made offerings to it, bowing down and worshiping this mass of wood and metal as an idol. Their bodies were reconfigured by the Nehushtan: knees bent, eyes up, hands extended in worship. Their souls were twisted by mere metal and wood: fears fixed on superstition, hearts bent away from God, trust turned to idols. Israel's beliefs and behaviors were reshaped by this piece of technology.

What makes the whole thing more tragic is that God intended for this pole to be a sign pointing to Jesus. Jesus told Nicodemus, "As Moses lifted up the serpent in the wilderness, so must the Son of Man be lifted up, that whoever believes in Him may have eternal life" (John 3:14–15). This created thing that was intended to direct Israel's gaze toward God and prefigure Jesus was instead used as an idol. In the process, hearts and minds were wrested away from fearing, loving, and trusting in God above all else.

The point is that humans can easily turn God's good gifts into idols. Created things have the power to change individuals and communities. People are transformed—positively or negatively—by the things that they use.

That was then. This is now. Can Instagram and Twitter become idols? Do smartphones and tablets, wearable devices and virtual assistants have the power to shape our minds and souls? Can we really be transformed by modern technology? Are you a different person as a result of your technology usage?

A DIFFERENT PERSON: RESEARCH ON HOW TECHNOLOGY CAN CHANGE US

Imagine that you could gather a dozen researchers from different disciplines. This group of researchers—sociologists and psychiatrists, theologians and anthropologists, computer engineers and communication scientists—would go about their research in radically different ways. Each researcher would employ distinct research methodologies, rely on different tools, and cite varying authorities. In one sense, these researchers would agree with one another on very little.

But they would likely all agree on one thing: technology has the power to change us. We become different people through

75

sustained technology use. Researchers from an array of disciplines have concluded that using technology results in marked changes in how we think, act, believe, feel, and live. Below are some examples of research into how technology changes users.

Envy

Scrolling through social media posts is a favorite pastime for many people. This activity is seemingly as innocuous as flipping through the pages of a book or taking a leisurely stroll. However, research has found that ambling through social media posts can increase our feelings of envy. A review of several research projects on the topic has found that social media use correlates with measurable increases in both envy and depression.[17] Other researchers have concluded that the feelings of envy experienced on social media platforms can take two different forms: malicious envy or benign envy.[18]

Malicious envy, as the name suggests, involves resentment and contempt toward another person. Malicious envy is often behind internet trolling, comment section slander, and hateful thoughts toward others. These sorts of actions are a way to cope with feelings of envy. So-called benign envy (a label developed by the researchers) involves admiration and a desire to obtain what the other person possesses. Researchers claim that this sense of envy spurs individuals to be more like the person who is being envied, rather than trying to bring others down.

According to the research, the closer the relationship, the more likely one is to have feelings of benign envy instead of malicious envy. When a close friend shares a post about running

17   Helmut Appel, Alexander L. Gerlach, and Jan Crusius, "The Interplay between Facebook Use, Social Comparison, Envy, and Depression," *Current Opinion in Psychology* 9 (June 2016): 44–49, https://doi.org/10.1016/j.copsyc.2015.10.006.
18   Ruoyun Lin and Sonja Utz, "The Emotional Responses of Browsing Facebook: Happiness, Envy, and the Role of Tie Strength," *Computers in Human Behavior* 52 (November 2015): 29–38, https://doi.org/10.1016/j.chb.2015.04.064.

a marathon, this may cause us to admire our friend and desire to emulate her. However, when a stranger shares the same post, this may cause us to criticize the individual as needlessly boasting about her accomplishments and seeking undue attention. However, any form of internet-induced envy is in direct conflict with God's desire for us to love one another: "Love does not envy or boast; it is not arrogant" (1 Corinthians 13:4).

Exposure

Research shows that technology can reshape individuals through exposure to sights and sounds, experiences and interactions. For example, virtual reality has been shown to activate the brain in ways that resemble real experiences.[19] The brain struggles to differentiate the difference between a person actually walking across a suspension bridge or just simulating it through a virtual reality headset.

Since digital technology can expose users to vivid experiences, it is being used in some surprising ways. Virtual reality can help medical students practice surgical operations, language learners experience what it is like to be immersed in a foreign country, and soldiers train for dangerous missions. Cognitive behavioral therapy (CBT) utilizes virtual reality safely to expose individuals to their fears in order to decrease phobias. These are all positive examples of how technology can be used to expose individuals to new and generative experiences.

On the other hand, technology can expose individuals to a plethora of violence, pornography, racism, and hatred. For instance, mounting evidence surrounds the risks associated with exposure to violence on television, websites, and video games.

---

19   Giuseppe Riva, Brenda K. Wiederhold, and Fabrizia Mantovani, "Neuroscience of Virtual Reality: From Virtual Exposure to Embodied Medicine," *Cyberpsychology, Behavior, and Social Networking* 22, no. 1 (January 2019): 82–96, https://doi.org/10.1089/cyber.2017.29099.gri.

Decades of research suggests that in general, people who are exposed to electronic media violence are also more aggressive.[20] However, researchers disagree on whether this is correlative or causative. Some researchers contend that greater exposure to media violence is linked to increases in aggression; other researchers believe that use of violent media is a symptom, and not the cause, of the aggressive nature of the individual.[21] However, it comes as no surprise that those who produce the violent media programs tend to downplay their influence on human behavior. Any way you slice it, individuals with more exposure to violent media are more violent in general, and at least one study found that playing violent electronic games is the strongest risk factor for violent crime.[22]

What makes things confusing is that most people who consume violent media are not violent; the consumption of violent media does not *predict* violence. However, individuals who consume heavy amounts of violent media, especially graphic violence, are at higher risk of being violent. How does this work? It seems most likely that just as some individuals cannot handle alcohol, some individuals are predisposed through individual characteristics or life situations to have difficulty handling violent media. It may bring out the worst in them. Picture each person like a row of dominoes, and things in our environment, including exposure to violent media, may knock over the dominoes, setting something bad into motion.

The risk of becoming violent from playing violent video

20 L. Rowell Huesmann, "The Impact of Electronic Media Violence: Scientific Theory and Research," *Journal of Adolescent Health* 41, no. 6, supplement (December 2007): S6–S13, https://doi.org/10.1016/j.jadohealth.2007.09.005.

21 Brad J. Bushman and Craig A. Anderson, "Media Violence and the American Public: Scientific Facts versus Media Misinformation," *American Psychologist* 56, no. 6–7 (June–July 2001): 477–89, https://doi.org/10.1037/0003-066x.56.6-7.477.

22 Werner H. Hopf, Günter L. Huber, and Rudolf H. Weiss, "Media Violence and Youth Violence: A 2-Year Longitudinal Study," *Journal of Media Psychology* 20, no. 3 (July 2008): 79–96, https://doi.org/10.1027/1864-1105.20.3.79.

games can be likened to the risk of being bitten by a shark. Playing Scrabble is like swimming in a pond where chances of a shark bite are slim to none. Playing violent video games is like swimming in the ocean; most people do not get bitten by sharks, but sharks do live in the ocean, and they do bite. Despite the research being inconclusive, the safest approach involves cautious, monitored media exposure and consumption.

Pride

Instagram, Pinterest, Facebook, and other social media platforms are often used as the highlight reel of people's lives. The content is curated and cropped, filtered and fixed up. People rarely post about messy living rooms, mounting debts, or muddled relationships. These digital trophy cases of words and photos make everyone else's life look really, really good. Digital time lines, walls, and pinboards are jammed with success stories, great accomplishments, new jobs, and five-minute miles. While our friends display their successes on social media, we are out there in the real world just trying to get a participation ribbon. No wonder we walk away from these places with our hearts full of envy.

Pride and envy are interwoven. Researchers have explored the relationship between envy and pride in digital spaces and found that self-promotion—pride, boasting, humblebragging—is a way that people try to deal with feelings of envy. According to the researchers, social media users employ an envy-coping strategy in which feelings of envy are offset by self-promotion and prideful boasting. It works in this way: an individual scrolls through social media posts, sees the successes of others, and becomes envious. As a way to manage these feelings of envy, this individual will share posts about his or her own successes and engage in prideful self-promotion. Others see these posts, become envious, and engage in similar behaviors. The researchers observing this phenomenon called it the "self-promotion-envy spiral." [23]

Humblebrags and Instagram-perfect pictures do not just randomly show up on your feeds. Rather, these prideful posts abound on the internet because of the sinful envy and pride within us all: "For all that is in the world—the desires of the flesh and the desires of the eyes and pride of life—is not from the Father but is from the world" (1 John 2:16). Digital technology powerfully plays upon the desires of the flesh and pride of life. The drive to worship becomes perverted, turning away from God and directed inward.

Distraction

A distraction is something that prevents full attention from being given to something else. Technology can prevent us from giving our full, undivided attention to meaningful thoughts and activities. Technology can become a barrier to living with godly purpose. Being distracted is also defined as a state of agitation of the mind; a distracted mind is one that is not at peace. These days, a multitude of technological advancements scream for our attention, reducing the attention we can give to any one thing. When we end up attending to or doing more than one thing at a time, we are multitasking. Our brains are not built to focus on more than one thing at a time. Multitasking creates increased stress on our brains. This increased mental effort is called cognitive load, and multitasking overwhelms the system.[24]

---

23 Hanna Krasnova, Helena Wenninger, Thomas Widjaja, and Peter Buxmann, "Envy on Facebook: A Hidden Threat to Users' Life Satisfaction?" (presented at the 11th International Conference on Wirtschaftsinformatik, Leipzig, Germany, February 27, 2013) 12, https://www.researchgate.net/publication/256712913_Envy_on_Facebook_A_Hidden_Threat_to_Users'_Life_Satisfaction.

24 Janina A. Hoffmann, Bettina von Helversen, and Jörg Rieskamp, "Deliberation's Blindsight:

A multitasking brain completes tasks more slowly and with more errors. Lending equal importance to all tasks, even meaningless ones such as scrolling through Facebook, results in being off task at times for all tasks. Distractions are unhealthy in the long-term, such as diminished learning from constant inattention, and in the short-term, such as the deadly consequences of texting while driving.

Why do we multitask? Multitasking is an illusion. It makes us look and feel more productive. Eventually, after the tasks are completed, the individual mistakenly assumes that the tasks were completed because of multitasking. The opposite is true; the tasks were impeded because of multitasking. Are teenagers more capable of multitasking because they all do it all the time? No, even their young, modern brains are not capable of focusing on more than one task at a time. The more you multitask, the more distracted you are. Research has demonstrated that you do not get better at multitasking by doing it more.[25] In our culture, there are many unhealthy behaviors that we mistakenly assume everyone is doing. You were not built for multitasking. These technological distractions are a product of humankind, not of God.

Depression

Whether it is a running app on your smartphone, a post on Reddit, or a group conversation on Facebook messenger, these platforms allow users to like, favorite, or upvote content. While this may appear to be inconsequential, those little blue thumbs and heart-shaped buttons have a tremendous power over us. Often, people use the number of likes to judge others

How Cognitive Load Can Improve Judgments," *Psychological Science* 24, no. 6 (June 2013): 869–79, https://doi.org/10.1177/0956797612463581.

25 M. Moisala et al., "Media Multitasking Is Associated with Distractibility and Increased Prefrontal Activity in Adolescents and Young Adults," *NeuroImage* 134, no. 1 (July 2016): 113–21, https://doi.org/10.1016/j.neuroimage.2016.04.011.

and themselves. Like buttons, favorites, and upvotes and down-votes are publicly quantifiable measures of social support.[26] According to research, the like button is a way to compare oneself with others. Like a human stock market, the number of likes makes social support quantifiable—and painfully public. How likable are you? Just take a look at the number of blue thumbs next to your photo. Are you as well-liked as your peers? Simply count your followers and compare that with others. This is a dangerous game.

It is not surprising, therefore, that depression can accompany social media use. Brain circuits that are used repeatedly are strengthened—sort of like how muscles are developed, except through a process of synaptic activity called *long-term potentiation*. Positive thinking strengthens healthy circuits; negative thinking strengthens unhealthy ways of thinking. Depressed thought patterns can be developed through this mechanism. Eventually, you can develop what is known as the cognitive triad of depression, with a pattern of negative thoughts about yourself, the world around you, and your future. As understood in cognitive behavioral therapy, developed by the influential psychiatrist Aaron Beck, our thoughts influence our emotions and behaviors.

The process may go something like this: You post a picture of yourself standing by the new car that you just purchased. You wait for the likes to come flowing in. Instead, in comes a trickle. You have an instant thought: no one likes me. This may be followed by increasingly damaging thoughts about your character that cut even deeper: I am unlikable. I am unlovable. These thoughts trigger feelings of sadness. It is hard to cope with your

---

26 Astrid M. Rosenthal-von der Pütten et al., "'Likes' as Social Rewards: Their Role in Online Social Comparison and Decisions to Like Other People's Selfies," *Computers in Human Behavior* 92 (March 2019): 76–86, https://doi.org/10.1016/j.chb.2018.10.017.

feelings of sadness. You reach for a bottle of wine and start shopping for your next major purchase.

The effects of social media on mood are often insidious. As we said earlier, no one has posted to Instagram and spontaneously combusted on the spot. People are more likely to think, "I am unhappy, but I don't know why." Millions of people use social media multiple times a day, and most engage with it without developing clinical depression that requires therapy or medication. This may be why research on how social media use affects mood often yields mixed results, and again the questions of correlation versus causation should be considered. Some users develop a big problem with social media use and its negative effects on their mood, whereas the rest leave a little bit sadder, angrier, and more anxious after exposure to social media.

It may not be a coincidence that we have seen significant increases in adolescent depression and suicide following the advent of social media. But social media platforms are not all bad; once again, the medical research is a mixed bag. Social media use does yield some positive benefits, including positive interpersonal connections, which may protect against some of the negative aspects of social media exposure. In other words, the benefits of social media may counterbalance the negatives.

The factors that seem to lead to the negative mood changes involve excessive time spent on social media and the quality of use of social media.[27] If we avoid using these platforms in excess, they become far less dangerous to our well-being. Similarly, upward social comparison on social media—comparing oneself to those who appear to be more successful—is associated with

---

27 Betul Keles, Niall McCrae, and Annmarie Grealish, "A Systematic Review: The Influence of Social Media on Depression, Anxiety and Psychological Distress in Adolescents," *International Journal of Adolescence and Youth* 25, no. 1 (March 2019): 79–93, https://doi.org/10 .1080/02673843.2019.1590851.

increases in depression and may be driven by envy;[28] therefore, consciously avoiding these sorts of social comparisons is one way to mitigate these issues. However, this is all easier said than done.

When it comes to social media, moderation is essential. It is important to use social media in moderation and to reflect on the proper use of this communication tool. When performed in excess and driven by anxieties such as obsessive-compulsive disorder, even prayer can lose its intended purpose and become unhealthy. For healthier social media use, researchers have found that limiting social media use to thirty minutes or less per day improved well-being with decreased depression, anxiety, and FOMO ("fear of missing out").[29]

REPENTANCE AND RENEWAL

This chapter has explored how technology can powerfully change us. Technology can lead to a metamorphosis in users, literally a change in form as it relates to thinking, feeling, behaving, and being.

Franz Kafka's novella *The Metamorphosis* explores the theme of transformation and what happens when someone is rapidly reshaped. The book begins in the most peculiar way: "One morning, when Gregor Samsa woke from troubled dreams, he found himself transformed in his bed into a horrible vermin."[30] Gregor, an otherwise healthy young man, had inexplicably become a bug. This metamorphosis set off a troubling sequence of

---

28 Wei Wang et al., "Upward Social Comparison on Mobile Social Media and Depression: The Mediating Role of Envy and the Moderating Role of Marital Quality," *Journal of Affective Disorders* 270 (June 2020): 143–49, https://doi.org/10.1016/j.jad.2020.03.173.

29 Melissa G. Hunt et al., "No More FOMO: Limiting Social Media Decreases Loneliness and Depression," *Journal of Social and Clinical Psychology* 37, no. 10 (December 2018): 751–68, https://doi.org/10.1521/jscp.2018.37.10.751.

30 Franz Kafka, *Metamorphosis*, trans. David Wyllie, chapter 1, Project Gutenberg, May 13, 2002, https://www.gutenberg.org/files/5200/5200-h/5200-h.htm.

events: his family did not know what to do, he lost his job as a salesman, and nearly everyone was afraid of him.

Curiously, Gregor was largely unaware that this transformation had occurred. When he awoke, he was immediately aware that he had changed; however, he only gradually became aware of how much he had truly changed. For example, a manager from his company came to the house trying to figure out why Gregor had missed work. Locked in his bedroom, Gregor spoke to the manager, saying, "I'll open up immediately, just a moment. I'm slightly unwell, an attack of dizziness, I haven't been able to get up. I'm still in bed now. I'm quite fresh again now, though. I'm just getting out of bed. Just a moment. Be patient!"[31] Outside the bedroom door stood Gregor's parents and the manager. After Gregor had finished speaking to them, the manager said to the parents, "Did you understand a word of all that?"[32] Gregor was entirely unaware that his voice had become just as insectile as his body.

Gregor's transformation was a catalyst for other transformations. The entire Samsa family—his father, mother, and sister—were all changed as a result of his transformation. After Gregor became a bug, the rest of the family experienced an emotional, relational, and financial metamorphosis. His transformation transformed the whole family.

Kafka's strange story can serve as a cautionary tale for technology use. Just as Gregor was initially unaware of his transformation, we may not always be aware of how technology is changing us. Often technology changes users in slow and subtle ways. It is hard to determine the extent to which our envy, pride, and distractedness are increasing. Likewise, it is not always apparent that our well-being, patience, and contentment

---

31   Kafka, chapter 1.
32   Kafka, chapter 1.

are decreasing. Occurring at the slow speed of fruit ripening on the vine, technology has the power to slowly—yet decisively—transform us.

Additionally, the transformations that happen through our technology use do not impact us alone. Just as Gregor's metamorphosis altered his entire family, a technology-induced metamorphosis alters more than just an individual. What was initially a novel sight—one person staring at a screen, walking down the sidewalk, and talking through a Bluetooth earpiece as though responding to voices in their head—becomes the new normal. Herds of teens, together but apart, are mesmerized by individual black mirrors while laughing to themselves. Whether it is a video game addiction, a habit of viewing pornography, obsessive email checking, or compulsive social media scrolling, these transformations affect others. Relationships, families, and communities are changed when individuals are changed.

Transformation abounded in the ministry of Jesus. Rather than using the word *metamorphosis*, Jesus often used the word *metanoia* and other closely related words. The Greek word *metanoia* is often translated as "repentance," meaning to turn away from sin. However, metanoia is also about transformation. When Jesus talked about metanoia, He was talking about the transformation that comes with receiving a new heart, a new mind, and a new way of being.

Jesus began His public ministry talking about metanoia, saying, "Repent, for the kingdom of heaven is at hand" (Matthew 4:17). And Jesus concluded His public ministry talking about metanoia, saying, "Thus it is written, that the Christ should suffer and on the third day rise from the dead, and that repentance for the forgiveness of sins should be proclaimed in His name to all nations, beginning from Jerusalem" (Luke

24:46–47). The ministry of Jesus is a ministry of metanoia, a ministry of transformation.

Jesus brings about transformation in us. Through His life, death, and resurrection, Jesus transforms us from dead sinners and brings us to life by the power of the Holy Spirit. In a beautiful reversal of Kafka's story, Jesus transforms us from horrible bugs into human beings made in the image of God. Rather than waking up to find that we have become horrible vermin, God awakens us through faith in Christ Jesus to become His holy people.

Metamorphosis by technology calls for metanoia from God. Technology does not improve us. We are made perfect in the likeness of God. These devices transform us in a way that does not reflect God. Human-made technology reflects the worst in us. The Holy Spirit transforms hearts, minds, and souls so that sinners become new creations in Christ Jesus: "The old has passed away; behold, the new has come" (2 Corinthians 5:17). The Holy Spirit accomplishes transformation in our lives through Baptism and hearing the Word of God. Baptism transforms us so that "as many of you as were baptized into Christ have put on Christ" (Galatians 3:27). God's Word transforms us as God has promised that it will: "So shall My word be that goes out from My mouth; it shall not return to Me empty, but it shall accomplish that which I purpose, and shall succeed in the thing for which I sent it" (Isaiah 55:11). God's gift of repentance and renewal in and through Jesus Christ is the only true hope for those who have been negatively transformed by technology.

The Christian response to technology-induced transformation is repentance. As Martin Luther stated in the first of his Ninety-Five Theses, "Our Lord and Master Jesus Christ, when He said, 'repent,' intended that the whole life of believers should be one of repentance."[33] Serious technology addictions, keyboard-punching people on Twitter, digital adultery, and iPhone idolatry require repentance. Subtle technology addictions, quietly envying Facebook friends, unspoken judgments that never end up in the comment section, and the endless pursuit of new gadgets require repentance. No matter who you are and what your relationship is to technology, we all need daily repentance. And we all need to hear the transformative word of Jesus: "Your sins are forgiven" (Matthew 9:2; Luke 7:48; see also John 20:23).

CONCLUSION

Technology, made by the design of humans and not directly by God, is released into the world regardless of the consequences, seen and unforeseen. One of the biggest dangers of technology is its power to change us. Some of this reshaping of minds and souls takes place through envy, exposure to sinful behaviors and attitudes, pride, distraction, and self-centeredness. Transformed in negative ways by the technology of the world, we need repentance and renewal through Christ to reshape us back into His image.

---

33 Martin Luther, *95 Theses* (St. Louis: Concordia Publishing House, 2016).

DISCUSSION QUESTIONS

1. How does digital technology shape our thoughts? How does it shape our feelings?

2. Think of one example of how digital technology shapes you or those around you in each of the following specific ways: envy, exposure, pride, distraction, and self-centeredness.

3. How are the creations of humankind different from those of the Creator in terms of design and effect?

4. How can repentance and renewal through Christ reshape us?

DO THIS, NOT THAT

TRUTH OVER DECEPTION

Deception and truth are opposed to each other. Scripture makes this clear in 1 John 1:8–9: "If we say we have no sin, we deceive ourselves, and the truth is not in us. If we confess our sins, He is faithful and just to forgive us our sins and to cleanse us from all unrighteousness." Deception declares falsehood by claiming to be without sin. Truth says it like it is, and God meets us with His mercy and forgiveness.

Based on this chapter, consider the following points for reflection or action as a way to flee from deception and embrace the truth:

- Consider the primary ways you use digital technology. Then consider the ways in which digital technology uses you. In what ways does social media control and influence you? How would your life look different without digital technology?

- Avoid using technology for technology's sake. Use technology with godly purpose. On a piece of paper, rank the primary ways in which you use digital technology from most to least necessary. Put together some steps that you might take to eliminate the least necessary forms of digital technology use from your life.

- Reflect on the original aims and purposes of digital technology as well as the unintended side effects of this creation. Knowing what we know now, if we had a do-over, what changes would we make to the creation of digital technology and how we use it?

- Ask yourself, "How would I know if technology is a problem for me?" More specifically, examine whether you have a problem with digital technology changing you in the areas covered in this chapter: envy, exposure (to violence, pornography, racism, and hatred), pride, distraction, and depression.

Implement these guidelines for daily living, including in your technology use:

- Do one thing at a time.

- Prioritize meaningful activities over distractions.

- Practice mindfulness, focusing on the present moment with godly purpose.

- Do not use social media as your main source of pleasure or coping. Do not deal maladaptively with toxic aspects of this real world by turning to toxic aspects of the digital world.

- For adults, limit social media use to thirty minutes or fewer per day, and spend thirty minutes or fewer every other day reviewing digital news.

- For parents, become familiar with and follow the guidelines from the American Academy of Pediatrics for children's digital media use. These guidelines include screen time recommendations from early childhood through adolescence. See also the discussion of media-free times and media-free locations as well as online citizenship and safety.

CHAPTER 5

TEMPTATION
AND TECHNOLOGY

Design is never neutral. It is a form of persuasion and communication, influencing our thoughts, feelings, perception, and actions. Design can even have life-and-death consequences.

The tragic explosion of the *Challenger* space shuttle in 1986 is an example of how design influences behavior (or in this case, fatal inaction). On January 28, 1986, the *Challenger* disintegrated just seventy-three seconds into flight. All seven passengers in the space shuttle died. Following the explosion, NASA determined that O-ring seals in the solid rocket booster had failed because of exceptionally cold temperatures on launch day.

But the O-rings weren't the only things to fail. Before that, a poorly designed chart failed to convince NASA to delay the launch. On the day of the launch, the temperature was forecasted to be 30 degrees Fahrenheit. Engineers from the company that manufactured the O-rings argued emphatically against launching the shuttle in such cold weather. They used a chart (see figure 4) to depict O-ring failure in previous test launches.

The chart shows the data in the order in which the tests were conducted. Shown in this way, it takes considerable effort to recognize that the colder the temperature, the more frequently the O-rings failed. Had the data been organized differently to make the correlation between temperature and O-ring failure more obvious, then it would have been abundantly clear that launching the shuttle at 30 degrees would be disastrous.

Edward Tufte, in his book *Visual Explanations: Images and Quantities, Evidence and Narrative*, has described this depiction of data as *chartjunk* because of its poor design and inability to communicate the danger of launching at colder temperatures. The visual depictions of the rockets are largely unnecessary and obscure the main concern of temperature and O-ring failure. The key that explained what each symbol meant was shown on a previous slide, which made the data more difficult to interpret. The chart shows *where* the O-ring failed but obfuscates the reason *why* the O-ring failed. Had the engineers designed the chart differently, as shown in figure 5 from a report prepared after the disaster, they might have convinced NASA to delay the flight.

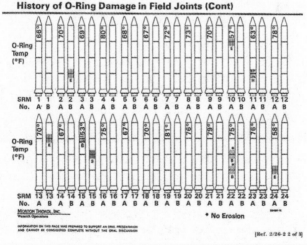

FIGURE 4. Original chart displaying O-ring failure. Image courtesy of NASA, *Report of the Presidential Commission on the Space Shuttle Challenger Accident*, vol. 5, p. 896, https://history.nasa.gov/rogersrep/v5p896.htm.

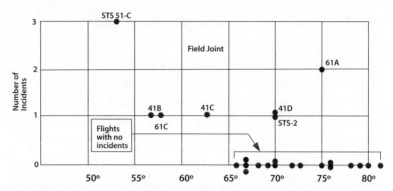

FIGURE 5. Redesigned chart of O-ring failure at lower temperatures. Image courtesy of NASA, *Report of the Presidential Commission on the Space Shuttle Challenger Accident*, vol. 1, p. 146, https://history.nasa.gov/rogersrep/v1ch6.htm#6.3.

Following the *Challenger* explosion, the Nobel Laureate physicist Richard Feynman designed an even simpler way to demonstrate the risk of a cold-weather launch. Feynman took one of the O-rings, placed it in ice water for a few seconds, and then took it out, revealing how it had become rigid and dented, unable to seal at colder temperatures. This simple experiment proved to be very persuasive as it clearly communicated the correlation between temperature and O-ring failure.

Design has consequences. In the case of the *Challenger* explosion, the problem went beyond rubber O-rings that were not designed for cold weather. Rather, the *Challenger* explosion hinged on poorly designed charts unable to persuade NASA officials to postpone the launch. Although it is not always obvious, design directs our thoughts, feelings, perception, and actions. Design is far more influential than is readily apparent. Therefore, design must be evaluated and understood.

DESIGNED FOR SIN

Technology is designed for sin. Devices are made to exploit temptations. Gadgets prey upon sinful inclinations.

These statements may sound ludicrous. Claiming that technology is designed for sin sounds like the unreasonable stance of a Luddite. However, upon further exploration, it becomes apparent that technology is indeed designed for sin and made to exploit temptation. Designers themselves have recognized the veracity of these statements.

The field of design includes a concept known as user-centered design. According to user-centered design, it is vitally important to understand users when one is designing a piece of technology. The design process ought to be grounded in the wants and needs of real-life users. Growing out of user-centered design is a relatively new field of study known as user-experience design (UX).

UX researchers study users with the aim of understanding their wants, needs, and behaviors. For example, UX researchers will study how users interact with devices, apps, and platforms. How often does someone go on Instagram? What is the average length of time spent on this platform? What sort of content causes users to spend more time using this platform?

User research is behind nearly all the design decisions at Facebook, Instagram, Twitter, TikTok, and every other major social media platform. In fact, an entire department at Facebook is dedicated to human computer interaction and UX. Teams of people at these technology companies are dedicated to researching and finding ways to capitalize on the individual behaviors, thoughts, and impulses of users.

Technology companies study real users in order to create products that they like and use more often. That is far from scandalous or sinister. But that is not the end of it.

Donald Norman, an influential thinker in modern design and the founder of the user-centered design concept, has recognized how technology is actually designed for sin. Norman has acknowledged that technology accommodates and facilitates human sinfulness. In the foreword to Chris Nodder's book *Evil by Design: Interaction Design to Lead Us into Temptation*, Norman describes how design should account for human sin, temptation, and desire. Norman does not argue for this because he is an evil villain; rather, he argues that technology should be designed around real human behavior and desires. The principles of user-centered design indicate that good design comes from good understanding. If good design understands real users, then designers must consider the sinful desires of their users.

Chris Nodder, a human-computer interaction scholar and UX researcher, argues that designers should purposefully create interfaces that play upon the emotions of users and control their behavior. Like a puppeteer skillfully pulling the strings of the marionette, Nodder argues that designers should control user behavior by exploiting users' sinful tendencies such as pride, envy, or lust. In fact, Nodder organizes his book *Evil by Design* around the seven deadly sins of pride, sloth, gluttony, anger, envy, lust, and greed. Exploring these sins, Nodder explains how designers can purposefully engage them through the products that they design.

Twitter's heart-shaped button, Facebook's blue thumbs-up, and LinkedIn's clapping hands are all examples of technology preying upon our sinful tendencies. These buttons are not there by accident. They are deliberate design decisions. After doing extensive user research, a team of designers determined that these buttons—known as one-click affordances—prompt emotional responses from users.

The like button is there because of our deep longing to be adored by others. We want to be liked and loved, admired and applauded. Although it can be so slight that we hardly stop to think about it, these social media features do something for us: when people click the heart-shaped button, it makes us feel loved by others; getting a thumbs-up from others feeds our self-justification; receiving an image of clapping hands causes a small swell of pride. The strings of our pride, envy, and greed are delicately plucked with each post and notification.

Social media platforms are not the only digital technology designed to capitalize on sin. Video games are intricately designed to stimulate greed and an insatiable desire for more: designers use tokens, rewards, and level advancements to get players so hooked on the game that eventually these extrinsic motivators eclipse the intrinsic motivator of personal challenge. Smart speakers offer the tempting prospect of significance and power; virtual assistants must listen to our every word even when we are yelling across the room like an impetuous emperor or empress commanding our assistant to order pizza. Fitness trackers spit out little pride-inducing pellets of data so that our hearts swell along with our muscles.

Theology can help us understand why technology is designed for sin. Human depravity, original sin, and desire are perennial themes within Christian theology. Augustine and Martin Luther are known for describing the human condition as *incurvatus in se* ("curved inward on oneself"). God made human creatures to be in a right relationship with Him, a relationship in which humans look to Him for all good things—life, identity, satisfaction, worth, protection, meaning, and goodness. Yet the human condition has been contorted by sin. Rather than living a life that is rightly aligned toward God and others, human sinfulness directs our life inward, toward self-justification, self-gratification, and self-aggrandizement. The notion that sin has warped, twisted, maimed, and ruined human goodness is as ubiquitous in theology as technology is in modern life.

Sin transforms human hearts so that they are curved inward and always looking for opportunities to fill the insatiable desire for pride, lust, envy, greed, and power. Designers and user-experience researchers, working with the assumption that their creations should meet the wants and needs of real human users, create products that attempt to satisfy these inwardly focused desires. If "all have sinned and fall short of the glory of God," as Romans 3:23 says, then it is no surprise that many designers account for human sinfulness when creating products for the digital age.

Thankfully, sin and temptation do not have the last word. Jesus does. And Jesus has triumphed over sin and temptation so that in Him we can be alive and free.

DEAD TO SIN, ALIVE TO CHRIST

Robert Louis Stevenson's book *The Strange Case of Dr. Jekyll and Mr. Hyde* tells of a potion designed for sin. All that is sinful within a person—all the lust, greed, envy, and hate—can be gathered together by this potion. In turn, all that is good and right within a person is free to flourish.

Dr. Jekyll, the designer behind this peculiar potion, senses that he is "an incongruous compound" of good and evil.[34] Jekyll concocts a potion that will separate out his two natures so that Dr. Jekyll can be entirely good and an alter ego, Edward Hyde, can be entirely bad. This potion is quite literally designed for sin—and saintliness.

Stevenson's book preceded Sigmund Freud's influential

---

34 Robert Louis Stevenson, *The Strange Case of Dr. Jekyll and Mr. Hyde*, Project Gutenberg, October 31, 1992, https://gutenberg.org/files/43/43-h/43-h.htm.

structural model of the psyche. However, many people have since come to interpret Stevenson's characters in the light of Freud's theories: Edward Hyde embodies what is called the *id*, the rampant instinctual desires of humans. Dr. Jekyll represents what is called the *superego*, the morality of humans. In Freud's philosophy, the balancing agent between the instinctually sinful and the critical, moralizing aspects of humanity is called the *ego*. Within both literature and psychology, *The Strange Case of Dr. Jekyll and Mr. Hyde* has been hugely influential.

As the story goes, Jekyll consumes this potion and "hides" his evil side in Mr. Hyde. By drinking the potion, Jekyll could doff the body of the noted professor and put on the body of Edward Hyde. It was that simple—for a while.

However, it proved to be unsustainable. Hyde was far more evil than Jekyll ever imagined. The concentration of sin and evil within Hyde became frightening. After a while, Dr. Jekyll would spontaneously turn into Mr. Hyde without even taking the potion. The novel ends with a bleak word from Dr. Jekyll: "Here then, as I lay down the pen and proceed to seal up my confession, I bring the life of that unhappy Henry Jekyll to an end."[35]

In the story of Jekyll and Hyde, drinking the cup leads to the triumph of sin and evil. The potion and the ensuing evil are too strong for good to prevail. In the Gospel of Jesus Christ, however, it is exactly the other way around. Jesus drinks a cup and it leads to the triumph of life and mercy. Jesus and His sacrifice on the cross are too strong for evil to prevail.

Throughout His ministry, Jesus repeatedly mentioned a cup that He would eventually drink: "Jesus said to them, 'You do not know what you are asking. Are you able to drink the cup that I drink, or to be baptized with the baptism with which I

---

35 Stevenson, *Dr. Jekyll and Mr. Hyde*.

am baptized?'" (Mark 10:38). While in the Garden of Gethsemane, Jesus knelt down and prayed, "Father, if You are willing, remove this cup from Me. Nevertheless, not My will, but Yours, be done" (Luke 22:42).

This cup that Jesus talks about is a reference to several Old Testament passages. Some passages in the Old Testament refer to drinking from a cup of salvation and blessing—the Book of Psalms, for example: "I will lift up the cup of salvation and call on the name of the LORD" (Psalm 116:13). However, other Old Testament references depict a cup of wrath (Isaiah 51:17; Ezekiel 23:33). Drinking this cup entails facing punishment and confronting the wrath of God: "Wake yourself, wake yourself, stand up, O Jerusalem, you who have drunk from the hand of the LORD the cup of His wrath, who have drunk to the dregs the bowl, the cup of staggering" (Isaiah 51:17).

In Gethsemane, when Jesus speaks of drinking the cup, He alludes to this cup of wrath that He would drink down to the dregs on the cross. Although the sin was not His own, He willingly consumed it for us on the cross. He drank down this pernicious potion so that our cup can overflow with God's goodness and mercy (Psalm 23:5–6).

After drinking the cup, Jesus died and was buried in the tomb. Yet the story does not end there. No. Unlike the strange case of Jekyll and Hyde, the Gospel of Jesus Christ does not end in death with evil dancing over the grave. In Christ Jesus, victory and life, mercy and salvation, hope and love get the final word. The resurrection of Jesus is His victory over sin and death, evil and Satan, temptation and turmoil.

The One who survives the cup of suffering and death invites us to partake of a far better cup: Jesus "took a cup, and when He had given thanks He gave it to them, saying, 'Drink of it, all of you, for this is My blood of the covenant, which is poured out for many for the forgiveness of sins'" (Matthew 26:27–28). The cup of forgiveness gathers together all that is sinful within a person, nails it to the cross of Christ, and puts it to death. This cup refers to the blood of Christ received in Holy Communion and also to the broader gift of forgiveness that permeates the whole Christian life. This cup of forgiveness offers new and eternal life in Jesus.

The cup that Jesus offers truly transforms sinners, leaving them dead to sin and alive to God:

> Now if we have died with Christ, we believe that we will also live with Him. We know that Christ, being raised from the dead, will never die again; death no longer has dominion over Him. For the death He died He died to sin, once for all, but the life He lives He lives to God. So you also must consider yourselves dead to sin and alive to God in Christ Jesus. (Romans 6:8–11)

Being alive to God in Christ Jesus means that our primary shape is no longer *incurvatus*, curved and inwardly focused. Jesus resurrects, redesigns, and reworks us so that we are new creations. Being alive to God in Christ Jesus transforms our relationship with both God and the world around us. In Jesus, we partake of the cup of salvation (Psalm 116:13), a cup that runs over with divine goodness (Psalm 23:5). The draught of salvation transforms our relationship with our Creator, other creatures, and that which has been created. We have died to sin and been made alive to Christ, and so our interactions with technology are transformed as well. Because we are truly alive and free in Jesus, technology loses its death grip on us.

STOP, FAST, SLOW

In Christ Jesus, we are new creations capable of new interactions with technology. The Holy Spirit dwells in us so that we are no longer enslaved to technologies that have been designed to exploit our sinful nature. We are alive and free. Therefore, we must reevaluate our interactions with technology as new creations in Christ. In order to do this, it is helpful to organize our interactions with various technologies into three broad categories: *stop*, *fast*, and *slow*.

Some interactions with technology are just plain sinful and need to stop. Some interactions with technology are beneficial but should be kept in check through periodic fasting or time away from them. And some interactions with technology are permissible, but we would benefit from slowing the frequency of our daily usage. Using technology with purpose involves asking a simple question: Do I need to stop, fast, or slow my use of this technology?

Stop

Certain uses of technology are unequivocally sinful. Any way you spin it, slice it, or say it—it is a sin. Internet pornography, social media infidelity, and swapping sexualized photos through text messaging are all obvious examples of sinful uses of technology. Yet many less obvious examples are sinful and need to stop. Hateful words posted on comment sections and blogs, bullying through group chats, and gossip in direct messages are sinful uses of technology. Stealing internet streaming services through password sharing or downloading content without paying for it also fits into this category.

Just because the designers of technology have made these sins easy to commit does not mean they are not really sins. They still are. And they must stop: "Wake up from your drunken stupor, as is right, and do not go on sinning" (1 Corinthians 15:34). People, especially youth, often mistakenly assume that as long as something is legal, it is not sinful. For example, pornography may be legal, but it is also sinful.

What begins as "just playing around" with sin can quickly turn into an addiction. Through the grace of Jesus and the power of the Holy Spirit, God frees us from our sin addiction. However, we often need help from people in our lives to change the sinful habits we have built. God uses spouses and friends, parents and pastors, advocates and medical professionals to help those in the midst of addiction.

Sinful uses of technology release dopamine in the brain. Dopamine causes pleasure, at least temporarily, but sin never satisfies for long. Instead, the brain learns to crave more and more dopamine, leading to an increase in the intensity and frequency of sinful use of technology.

If the brain's hunger for this dopamine is not satisfied, the sensation is highly uncomfortable. At first, when the urge to engage in behaviors involving a sinful use of technology is resisted, things may worsen. In the early stages of breaking a habit, the craving is most intense and the urges to return to the sources of this dopamine most compelling. This is called an extinction burst. This is commonly seen when a parent prevents a child from accessing a technological source of pleasure—for example, the video game Fortnite—and it results in a tantrum. The child is unable to cope with being cut off from his or her dopamine dealer and is overwhelmed by the unpleasant sensations that occur.

Since all sin should be avoided, there is no such thing as a "moderate amount" of sinful use of technology, as if viewing pornography for five minutes is not a sin, while viewing it for fifty minutes is a sin. Stopping cold turkey is often what is needed to break a habit. Withdrawal, the period immediately after cessation, is the most trying time with very unpleasant sensations and intense cravings for the object of desire. However, although withdrawal symptoms get worse before they get better, eventually it does get easier after a prolonged period.

With addictions, whether it is a drug or a technology, it is hard to take away something without putting something else in its place. Think of the beginning scene from *Raiders of the Lost Ark*. Indiana Jones steals a golden idol, swiping it from atop a stone pillar. But he doesn't put the right thing in its place (in this case, a bag of sand), and as a result, a large boulder comes crashing down toward him, steamrolling everything in its path. In the case of drugs, medications may assist in the treatment of withdrawal and maintenance of abstinence from the drug. In the case of sinful technology use, safeguards must be put in place to monitor and prevent access to sinful technology. But these measures are destined to fail unless something else takes the place of the sinful activity. When Jesus replaces the idols that sit upon hearts, sin will undoubtedly be crouching at the door of our hearts (Genesis 4:7). When stopping our sin addictions, it is wise to add something such as prayer, Bible reading, exercise, or meeting with an accountability partner.

Fast

Some of our interactions with technology are beneficial, yet ought to be fasted from on occasion. For example, emails or video meetings can be beneficial tools used in good and godly ways for the well-being of others. We may check email and conduct video meetings as part of our vocations. Similarly, time spent with laptops, tablets, smartphones, and VR headsets can be constructive and indeed good.

Yet even good things ought to be fasted from on a regular basis. God established a rhythm in creation when He worked for six days and rested on the seventh. This pattern of work and rest was reiterated by God in the command to keep the Sabbath:

> The seventh day is a Sabbath to the LORD your God. On it you shall not do any work, you or your son or your daughter or your male servant or your female servant, or your ox or your donkey or any of your livestock, or the sojourner who is within your gates, that your male servant and your female servant may rest as well as you. (Deuteronomy 5:14)

It is important to note that not only people are invited into this Sabbath rest but also oxen, donkeys, and livestock. These creatures were the livelihood tools of an agrarian society. Sabbath rest and fasting applied both to human creatures and to the tools that they used.

Laptops and digital devices are not living creatures the way the oxen, donkeys, and livestock are. However, these are indeed the tools that we use in our modern, technological society. Do we ever give these tools a rest? Do we ever take a day to fast from email, video meetings, and keyboards? Does your computer ever get turned off completely rather than just the temporary sleep mode? Although these tools can be good things used as part of our legitimate work and vocations, fasting can keep them in their rightful place within our lives.

Many things happen when we fast. Faith is strengthened by the Holy Spirit through fasting as we come to experience God's faithfulness. God provides for us even when we do not check our email for a day. God sustains us with all that we need even when our phone is on airplane mode. Additionally, we develop self-control by intentionally setting aside a day or time to fast from certain technologies (1 Corinthians 9:24–27).

But fasting offers more than just spiritual benefits. Fasting is a vital tool in both the prevention of and recovery from addiction. Fasting is the absence of a behavior or complete abstinence from it. On the other hand, compulsion is repeated behavior or the complete acceptance of it. They are opposites, and it makes perfect sense that one cannot develop a compulsive habit in the presence of fasting. Fasting also prevents the development of tolerance, in which a habit needs to increase in frequency and intensity in order to produce the same amount of pleasure as when it was first started. This concept is illustrated by the person with alcoholism who requires one case of beer to get drunk at age 25 and two cases to get drunk at age 35. This sort of tolerance is only developed through years of consistent alcohol use without any prolonged periods of fasting.

Through the process of fasting, tolerances can be reset so that smaller amounts of exposure to the old habit can once again produce pleasure. Fasting disciplines the body and enables real-life pleasures, such as food and companionship, to become pleasurable once again. Addictive pleasures have a bad habit of resetting our pleasure threshold so that the addictions are the only things in our lives that bring any pleasure, with their dopamine bursts much greater than those of natural life reinforcers. When addicted to drugs, a good meal doesn't bring pleasure and satisfaction as it once did; it does not even move the needle. Fasting keeps addiction in its place and allows us to enjoy God's good gifts as He intends.

Slow

Some interactions with technology are permissible, but we would benefit from decreasing or slowing our usage. Streaming videos or scrolling social media are good examples within this category. Assuming that the shows you watch or your social media interactions are not sinful, these usages of technology are permissible within the Christian life. Yet even though they are permissible and not sinful, the timeless wisdom of "less is best" holds true. As we hear in 1 Corinthians 6:12, "'All things are lawful for me,' but not all things are helpful. 'All things are lawful for me,' but I will not be dominated by anything."

Aggregate numbers—adding up the total of many days, months, or years—can be very informative. Imagine if you could know the total number of hours spent swiping your fingers upward while listlessly looking at cat memes. Imagine if there was a massive spreadsheet about your life documenting all the time you have spent bingeing on shows, checking emails, glancing at your phone, or pushing video game controls. Those aggregate numbers would be downright frightening.

In light of this, slowing our consumption and use of technology is wise. Very small changes repeated over long periods of time can have major consequences. Instead of 1 percent more each year, aim for 1 percent less. Instead of being an early adopter of new technologies, consciously seek to be a slow adopter with some technologies. Consider whether you really need all ninety inches of that new television. If your habit is always 1 percent more when it comes to technology, your habit is driven by greed and gluttony. This means that your habits surrounding technology may soon become habits of sin: "But I say, walk by the Spirit, and you will not gratify the desires of the flesh. . . . And those who belong to Christ Jesus have crucified the flesh with its passions and desires" (Galatians 5:16, 24).

As with fasting, developing habits of self-control will benefit more than just your soul. From a mental health standpoint, our self-control is limited when confronted by powerful forces such as drugs and digital technology or when we're in a highly emotional state. It is difficult to make wise choices in the middle of an urge or under the spell of intense emotions. We call this state *hot cognition*—thoughts and choices we make when we're not fully in control of ourselves and our emotions.

We're best able to control ourselves when we are calm and thinking clearly, when we are not immediately faced with intense cravings stimulated by the object of desire or strong emotions. Someone recovering from alcoholism must have the self-control not to return to his favorite watering hole; someone on a diet must have self-control to avoid purchasing big bags of chips while at the supermarket. Likewise, we need self-control to avoid harmful uses of digital technology. But we must work at this. Brain circuits are strengthened through use and weakened from lack of use. Planning to limit temptations and avoiding engagement with sinful technology strengthens the brain circuits for self-control and teaches the brain other ways to achieve pleasure.

The slower the interactions with digital technology, the more time we have to think about our actions. Thoughtfulness is the opposite of impulsiveness. With impulsive actions, we often later exclaim, "What was I thinking?" Well, you probably weren't thinking. This is especially true of binges. Binges are fast-paced with heavy amounts of consumption over short periods of time. Classically, we think of binges as involving food, alcohol, or drugs. However, it is also possible to binge on digital technology. We may intend to check one thing on our phones quickly, but the next thing we know, our eyes are glazed, our heads ache, and two hours have passed with the phone in our hands. A binge is the ultimate example of loss of self-control. The antidote to a binge is slow use of technology. Go ahead and watch every episode of that new show—just do it over the course of a year and not a weekend.

CONCLUSION

In order to fix a problem, you must first have awareness of the problem. The first step toward healthy use of digital technology is to realize that technology is often designed to exploit our sinful inclinations. But through the power of Christ, we are new creations, no longer enslaved by our sin and sinful habits. This means we can control our interactions with technology rather than let the created things control us. In order for this to happen, the followers of Jesus must discern their technology use and consider where they need to stop (avoid unequivocally sinful uses), fast (take healthy breaks), or slow (use in measured, deliberate ways).

DISCUSSION QUESTIONS

1. How is digital technology designed to cause temptation?

2. Which use of digital technology do you find most difficult to resist? Why?

3. Think of your own uses of digital technology. Which uses do you need to stop, fast, or slow? Create a specific plan for how to do this.

4. What is God's design for you? How is this sometimes at odds with how digital technology uses you?

DO THIS, NOT THAT

BREAK THE CHAINS

This chapter explored some of the ways technology tries to chain us to certain habits, behaviors, or patterns. Being free in Christ means not being chained to technology. Let's consider ways to break the chains technology has on us, using smartphones as an example.

Can you disconnect? Turn off your smartphone and put it away for an extended period of time. As they say when something is easy to do, "No problem." But if the answer is no—if you weren't able to put it away or cannot imagine stepping away from your smartphone—then there may be a problem. Feeling the need to have something ever present in your life implies dependence on that object. Sometimes, we are truly dependent on something; it's essential for life, such as the oxygen we breathe. However, smartphones are not essential for life. If you can't be away from your smartphone, then that dependence is a problem.

Try fasting. You can't fast from something if it is always part of you. Put some distance between yourself and your electronic devices. Fasting from your smartphone should be an ongoing practice.

- Physically put away the smartphone—not in your pocket, but in a drawer somewhere—and put Holy Scripture in its place. Without the constant mental white noise from the smartphone, less distraction interferes between you and God.

- Fast from your smartphone periodically throughout your day. Turn it off when not in use. If necessary, check it periodically throughout the day at regularly spaced-out intervals. When on your phone, limit your use to five minutes or less at a time.

- Fast from your smartphone one hour before bed. Your sleep may improve. Turn off notifications and other sounds that influence excessive checking of your phone. Do not become Pavlov's dog, conditioned by its design features so that you salivate at the sound of the bell. Do not respond to every text message immediately after it is received. Purposely delay returning these texts.

Interact thoughtfully. Fasting will help you develop self-control to interact more thoughtfully when you do use your smartphone.

- Do not respond to electronic communications when emotionally upset. Impulsive actions are done without first thinking about how to respond, but fasting will help you get in the practice of waiting to respond.

- Do not feel pressured to be always available and to respond immediately to electronic messages in an effort to reassure others or to avoid conflict; this type of behavioral pattern is not helpful or healthy. If others become upset about not immediately receiving responses from you, this reaction may be about them and their issues with digital technology.

Do a digital media audit. Earlier in this book, you were invited to do an audit of your technology use. Similar to that exercise, take an inventory of the ways you consume digital media. Choose one type of use to stop, one to fast from, and one to slow down.

- For example, do not be fooled into thinking you need to follow the twenty-four-hour news cycle. Slow your consumption of news to thirty minutes or less every other day.

- Figure out what you need to know about the news of the world and how much you need to know in order to be healthy. Most news does not pertain to our lives, we have little control over it, and it makes us fearful or angry.

Use common sense. There are always exceptions to these recommendations for breaking the chains of your smart-phone.

- Do not turn off your smartphone when expecting a call from your spouse to be picked up from the airport. (Do we really have to tell you that? We know that someone needs to hear it!)

- Take some time to obtain knowledge critically about major world events. You do not need to delete all your news apps or avoid them entirely. It is wise to be informed about what is going on in the world around you.

- Time your fasts purposefully. For example, you may be able to engage in a prolonged fast from your smartphone while on vacation. On a beach vacation

113

with your family, you may have the luxury of turning it off, putting it in a drawer, and taking it out one week later. The first few days are the hardest (as with any withdrawal), and then you may remember or get a taste of what life is like without smartphones.

By using our smartphones and other digital technologies thoughtfully and in moderation, we can grow mentally and spiritually. The best technology use is when we use it because we need to, unmotivated by temptation.

CHAPTER 6

DIGITAL NARCISSISM

"While he is drinking, being attracted with the reflection of his own form, seen in the water, he falls in love with a thing that has no substance; and he thinks that to be a body, which is but a shadow."[36]

Ovid's *Metamorphosis* recounts many ancient tales. Among the most well-known of these is the story of the self-absorbed young Narcissus. As the story goes, nobody loved Narcissus quite as much as Narcissus. Others tried to gain his attention, but their efforts were met with disdain and rejection.

Narcissus happened upon a spring of water while he was out hunting one day. Bending over to quench his thirst in this pool of water, Narcissus saw his reflection. Upon seeing this shadow of his own form, Narcissus could not bear to look away.

And so this self-centered love affair became a tragedy: "No regard for food, no regard for repose, can draw him away thence; but, lying along upon the overshadowed grass, he gazes upon the fallacious image with unsatiated eyes, and by his own sight he himself is undone."[37]

With blunt objectivity, Ovid describes the folly of Narcissus falling in love with a shadow, a fallacious image, a mere reflection. Narcissus staked his life on something that was without

---

36 Ovid, *Metamorphosis*, translated by Henry T. Riley, III.413–45, Project Gutenberg, http://www.gutenberg.org/files/21765/21765-h/files/Met_I-III.html#booklll_fableVI.

37 Ovid, *Metamorphosis*.

substance. Narcissus lived—and ultimately died—for something that was fleeting and fake.

UNDERSTANDING NARCISSISM

We all experience moments of narcissism—intense self-centeredness—especially during adolescence. The Greeks gave us the idea of navel-gazing, from the term *omphaloskepsis*, to describe these times of self-absorption. However, for some of us, narcissism can become chronic, persisting beyond our youth into adulthood. As described in the *Diagnostic and Statistical Manual of Mental Disorders*, narcissistic personality disorder is a pattern of pervasive and unchanging self-centeredness that causes suffering and impairment.[38] Narcissism is the antithesis of Christ. At its most extreme, narcissism becomes self-worship. Narcissism also involves the excessive pursuit of the admiration of others with the desire to become a living idol. Narcissistic people have unbridled personal ambition and lack empathy for others. Jesus was the embodiment of empathy—God sharing in the feelings of humanity.

Narcissism involves taking sole credit for personal accomplishments, not recognizing and acknowledging the contributions and gifts of others, including God. Narcissistic people feel superior to others, more special, and may focus on status, only wanting to spend time with those of high status. They would never associate with the meek or lowly. Extreme narcissism is driven by the dangerous desire to be godlike, with fantasies of unlimited power. Narcissistic people are envious of others and distrustful. Narcissism does not bring lasting happiness or fulfillment. It is often a defense against feeling bad about oneself.

---

38 American Psychiatric Association, *Diagnostic and Statistical Manual of Mental Disorders*, 5th ed. (Arlington, VA: American Psychiatric Association Press, 2013), 669–72.

However, this thin layer of bravado covering fragile and sensitive low self-esteem is easily breached. Narcissistic people react with despair and rage when they receive criticism, believe they have lost, or otherwise experience injury to their ego. Only hollowness and emptiness lie beneath the narcissism.

MEDIA
AND THE EXTENSION OF THE SELF

While it is not entirely obvious, the ancient tale of Narcissus has something to do with media. Narcissus loved how the reflective pool of water mediated a view of himself. This watery mirror served as a medium through which he could lovingly gaze upon his own image. This pool of water, which ultimately proved to be fatal, was by definition a form of media.

Media, the plural of *medium*, is anything through which something is communicated or expressed. A *medium* is that which conveys ideas, images, or information.

For example, visual artists use media such as clay, marble, or oil paint to convey creative ideas through sculptures or paintings. Writers use media such as words, sentences, and books to communicate concepts and stories. Musicians use instruments, digital devices, and audio recordings to deliver sounds to the world. All of these things—clay, books, and audio recordings—are forms of media.

Media surprisingly played a role in the tragic death of Narcissus. Had this marshy medium not extended his face beyond his nose, he might have been able to embrace someone other than himself. Had the reflective pool not communicated the reflection of his own form, then this would not be a cautionary tale retold throughout the ages.

One of the most influential thinkers on the topic of modern

media is Marshall McLuhan. In his book *Understanding Media: The Extensions of Man*, McLuhan describes how media can function as an extension of ourselves. According to McLuhan, human beings try to extend their bodies beyond their usual reach or ability. Individuals desire any material means of extending themselves beyond themselves. This may sound abstract at first, but it becomes rather obvious with just a few simple examples.

The foot is an easy way to think about how technology and media function as extensions of the human body. Stilts quite literally extend the human bones—the femur, fibula, tibia, metatarsals, and phalanges—and permit one to stand several feet taller than usual. Standing on stilts extends your legs and feet, extending your body by means of wooden sticks. The stilts, therefore, could be thought of as a medium of sorts, transferring the leg bone through the wood to the ground. Yet apart from the odd clown reading this book, not many of us walk around on stilts.

Many people get around by car, however. In a car, a human foot makes contact with the accelerator and brake pedals. The etymology of the word *pedal* is similar to the word *pedestrian*: both words are based on the Latin *pedes*, meaning "on foot." In a car, your actual foot touches a pedal, and it translates the movement of your foot through the pedal, through the drivetrain, and into the wheels. The human foot is extended by means of the pedal, engine, transmission, and wheels. In a way, the wheel is connected to the foot. The pedal, engine, transmission, and wheels become sorts of media transferring the movements of the foot to the ground. Only Fred Flintstone places his feet directly on the ground to control his vehicle.

The same is true for other parts of the body. For example,

human skin is extended by the clothing that we wear. Shirts and sweaters act as an extension of the flesh in order to maintain proper body temperature; the colder it is outside, the more layers or extensions of the self it takes to keep warm. Similarly, a household furnace and thermostat extend the work of the hypothalamus in the brain by externally regulating temperature. These pieces of technology are artificial extensions of the thermoregulation organs in the body.

Like stilts, wheels, and furnaces, digital media can be an artificial extension of us. Our physical profiles are reflected through digital profiles: Facebook allows our face to be viewed from afar. Zoom, Skype, and other teleconferencing technologies enable our voices and bodies to extend artificially across time zones and thousands of miles. Text messages and tweets extend our thoughts and ideas into the great digital beyond. Cameras capture our image and communicate it far beyond our physical bodies. Through digital media, our faces, voices, ideas, and bodies can stretch way beyond our physical bodies into digital realms.

McLuhan has a vivid way of describing how media extend various parts of our bodies: self-amputation. While it is certainly vivid—and a bit violent—it definitely gets the point across. Digital media enable a little part of you to be chopped away from the whole you and sent far, far away. Podcasts are disembodied voices. Selfies are soulless faces. Videos are bodies without weight or substance. Books are minds without bodies. Media capture one part of us while leaving the rest behind.

This self-amputation comes at a cost. As digital media extend parts of our bodies into other places, we can become fragmented and numb. Digital self-amputation leaves us feeling dismembered. While we may not often think of it like this, we have all experienced the dismembering effects of digital media.

Distantly Present

This trend has become one of the most ubiquitous phenomena in our modern times. A couple is out to dinner in a restaurant; both are physically together but miles away from each other on their phones. Their bodies may be in the same room, but their eyes and minds are miles away from each other. Similarly, a parent may be physically present with his or her child in the front yard or the park. And yet a news alert or email notification can instantly transport the mind halfway across the globe. Students walk across a college campus while engaged in a group text with friends from several different colleges. Our physical bodies may be in one place, but digital media cause us to be all over the place.

Commonly Senseless

Digital media destroy our common sense. This technology-induced loss of common sense is not a lack of practical wisdom such as "a stitch in time saves nine" or "a penny saved is a penny earned." Rather, digital media work against the unity of our bodily senses.

The ancient notion of *sensus communis*, from which the term "common sense" derives, has to do with the unity of our bodily senses. Discussions about the bodily senses appear in classical philosophical texts such as Plato's *Theaetetus* and Aristotle's *De Anima*. Other scholars such as Thomas Aquinas, John Locke, and Immanuel Kant all tried to make sense of how the bodily senses interact with one another. In the Small Catechism, Martin Luther talks about the bodily senses in the explanation of the First Article of the Apostles' Creed: "I believe that God has made me and all creatures; that He has given me my body and soul, eyes, ears, and all my members, my reason and all my senses, and still takes care of them."

While various scholars and theologians have differed on how they understand the *sensus communis*, they largely agree that our senses must work together in order to perceive and interpret the world around us. The communion of the bodily senses—touch, sight, hearing, smell, and so forth—are essential to our knowledge and perception. Yet our bodily senses are reoriented by technology and media. Different kinds of media prioritize one bodily sense over the other.

For example, a Zoom video call gives priority to sight and sound over other bodily senses, such as smell or touch, which are more heavily involved in face-to-face conversations. Using headphones to listen to an audio recording of a classical concerto gives priority to the ears, whereas the actual symphony hall involves seeing the musicians, feeling the sounds, and imbibing the fullness of the atmosphere. Digital media distort our common sense—the unity of all our senses—by giving priority to some of our bodily senses over and against our other senses.

Comfortably Numb

According to McLuhan, another consequence of our interaction with digital media is numbness. Rather than opening up the world, digital technology can gradually close off our senses and leave us comfortably numb, much like narcotic drugs. (In fact, *Narcissus* and *narcotic* share a common Greek etymological background.) Since we are all over the place, we lose the ability fully to see, feel, and taste or simply to be present in one place. We may see a picture-perfect sunset and compulsively grab our phone like a well-trained Pavlovian canine. Why? Because our friends a thousand miles away from that sunset might like to see a filtered version of what we are seeing. The pungent conifer smell experienced while on a hike is lost amid the compulsion to turn those pine trees into potential Instagram posts. The timbral tones of birdsong are deafened by earbuds blasting a Spotify playlist. The taste of food is deadened by the impulse to Snapchat the moment. Constant use of digital technology trains us to tune out of the present and lose the full experience of our senses.

An extreme version of this type of numbness is called depersonalization, which is seen in psychiatric conditions such as post-traumatic stress disorder (PTSD) and drug-induced states. But depersonalization may also be a consequence of filtering our lives through digital media. Humans can become disconnected and robotlike, experiencing their feelings, behaviors, and thoughts from a distance. Life becomes an out-of-body experience.

Oddly Narcissistic

Not only are we distantly present, largely senseless, and comfortably numb, but all these digital media also make us oddly narcissistic. Since we have so many different digital tools and technologies available to us, we spend a tremendous amount of time and effort using these tools to extend ourselves. Scripture warns against a life set on the self:

> For people will be lovers of self, lovers of money, proud, arrogant, abusive, disobedient to their parents, ungrateful, unholy, heartless, unappeasable, slanderous, without self-control, brutal, not loving good, treacherous, reckless, swollen with conceit, lovers of pleasure rather than lovers of God. (2 Timothy 3:2–4)

A life set on the self causes us to be lovers of the self—proud, arrogant, and swollen with conceit. Although digital media make these traits common, that does not make them right or good.

In a sense, digital media tempt us to be discontented with God's creation. Everything must be filtered and retouched. Fitness companies are now developing digitally enhanced mirrors that can visually alter one's body shape and appearance as a way to motivate exercise habits. Digital narcissism can lead some to distort their appearance willfully. Faces, bodies, and lives become unrecognizable; when all of this happens, we become unrecognizable. In extreme cases, body dysmorphia may develop. People with this condition are obsessed with perceived flaws in their appearance. In reality, they look normal or only have minor physical imperfections. A modern version of this has been termed "Snapchat dysmorphia." Patients are seeing doctors, plastic surgeons, who will make them look like their doctored images on digital media. Individuals with body dysmorphia may have dozens of surgeries but are never satisfied with the results. While these examples are extreme, digital media affect us all, fueling unrealistic expectations that can keep us from being content with the way God created us.

God did not make us for this kind of life. God's plan for human flourishing does not include being distantly present, commonly senseless, comfortably numb, and oddly narcissistic. Rather, God created human creatures for a wholly different way of living. God created His human creatures to be in real communion with Him and one another. God created us to be whole and present at one time and place so that we can experience real life, real community, and real relationships. By the grace of God, this has all become possible in and through Christ Jesus.

GOD: REAL, TRUE, ENDURING

No substance. A shadow. A "fallacious image." This is how Ovid described the watery grave that so gripped Narcissus. And this is how we should think of digital media. On the whole, it is an insubstantial shadow that disappears as soon as the power button is pressed or the battery runs out. When the Wi-Fi signal drops or the screen breaks, the image disappears. With heads down, backs bent, and eyes gazing at glowing rectangles, we give much of our time to shadows.

Scripture frequently mentions shadows. On many occasions, humans and humanly created things are likened to shadows. For example, Psalm 144:3–4 declares, "O LORD, what is man that You regard him, or the son of man that You think of him? Man is like a breath; his days are like a passing shadow." Psalm 102:11–12 offers a similar description: "My days are like an evening shadow; I wither away like grass. But You, O LORD, are enthroned forever; You are remembered throughout all generations."

Human creatures are in some sense like shadows. A shadow is ephemeral, fleeting, and disappears over time; similarly, our earthly days are limited and relatively short. The same can be said of humanly created things: Google+, YikYak, Vine, and countless other social media platforms came and went like shadows. Gadgets such as pagers and MiniDisc players disappeared in a matter of years. We often give far too much of our time and effort, focus and future to fleeting shadows. Longing for a little blue thumbs-up or a red notification bell that disappears the moment we touch it is the epitome of ephemeral. Exchanging months of sweat and hard work for a television that will be obsolete as soon as we take it out of the box is fleeting satisfaction. Gazing at photos that will ripple away into an algorithmic abyss is the modern version of Narcissus gazing into the pool of water. Human creatures spend far too much time fixated on that which is fleeting and disappearing.

God, however, remains.

God is far from fleeting or ephemeral. Scripture uses shadows in entirely different ways when it comes to God:

> Return, O Israel, to the LORD your God, for you have stumbled because of your iniquity. . . . They shall return and dwell beneath My shadow; they shall flourish like the grain; they shall blossom like the vine; their fame shall be like the wine of Lebanon. (Hosea 14:1, 7)

The shadow of the Lord is a place of refuge and respite (Psalm 121). Unlike the shadowy breath of our earthly days, God casts an enduring shadow because He is eternal.

Both God and the gifts that He gives do not disappear because of a power button or dead battery. Rather, "every good gift and every perfect gift is from above, coming down from the Father of lights, with whom there is no variation or shadow due to change" (James 1:17).

Jesus, God in human flesh, is equally enduring and eternal. In an evanescent world, Jesus is forever:

> He is the image of the invisible God, the firstborn of all creation. For by Him all things were created, in heaven and on earth, visible and invisible, whether thrones or dominions or rulers or authorities—all things were created through Him and for Him. And He is before all things, and in Him all things hold together. And He is the head of the body, the church. He is the beginning, the firstborn

> from the dead, that in everything He might be pre-eminent. For in Him all the fullness of God was pleased to dwell, and through Him to reconcile to Himself all things, whether on earth or in heaven, making peace by the blood of His cross. (Colossians 1:15–20)

All of this is to say that "the substance belongs to Christ" (Colossians 2:17). Jesus is the fullness of God. Substantial power belongs to Him: He speaks and dead people arise (Luke 7:11–17). He breaks bread, and eyes open (Luke 24:30–32). He shatters the bonds of sin (Luke 5:20). He proclaims "good news to the poor" and "liberty to the captives" (Luke 4:16–22). He died on a cross and, three days later, rose in victory (John 20).

Promised by God in the beginning, heralded by the prophets of Israel, and announced by the heavenly host, Jesus is God Incarnate. The Gospels do not depict Jesus as a hologram, an avatar, or a virtual representation. In no way is Jesus portrayed as a shadow, a fallacious image, or a mere reflection, as in the story of Narcissus. Instead, the biblical narrative tells of Jesus being fully human—God enfleshed with muscle and bone, sinew and blood, skin and sweat, hair and fingernails. Jesus is as real as it gets.

His birth, like all births, involved blood and pain. He walked real, dusty streets of real places such as Nazareth, Galilee, and Jerusalem. He touched the gnarled and ulcerous skin of untouchable lepers. He wept real tears at the tomb of Lazarus. And Jesus permitted real nails to pierce His skin as warm, crimson blood flowed forth.

Shadows come and go. Shadows disappear. Shadows have no weight or substance. But unlike shadows, God remains. God was, is, and will be: "'I am the Alpha and the Omega,' says the Lord God, 'who is and who was and who is to come, the Almighty'" (Revelation 1:8). Jesus, the incarnate Son of God, is weighty and substantial—real reality. The Holy Spirit also comes to us in real and substantial ways: the Word of God, Baptism, Holy Communion, and the Church.

In a world that is full of mirages and mirrors, screens and shadows, God anchors us in that which is real and physical, eternal and enduring.

RESISTING DIGITAL NARCISSISM

While this chapter argues that digital media are like a fleeting shadow or a weightless reflection, don't mistake that for a complete lack of realness or physicality. The internet, digital media, and social media are in many ways real and physical. Actual wires and cables permit real bits of data to travel around the world. In fact, massive subaquatic cables stretch across the oceans so that emails can be sent between continents. Although it's not always obvious, social media platforms involve real and physical people on both ends of the interface. (It's always good to remember that you are interacting with a real person on the other end of the computer before you keyboard-punch someone on Twitter.) Furthermore, real companies and people create and maintain social media platforms and interfaces. Cyberbullying, internet addictions, and digital distractions come with real-life consequences.

Along these same lines, digital media actually have weight. Well, kind of. According to John Kubiatowicz, a computer science professor at the University of California, the difference between a completely empty and a fully loaded 4GB Kindle e-reader is a billionth of a billionth of a gram—that's 0.000000000000000001 grams. (This is only theoretically established, since scales are not able to measure this extremely slight change in weight.) Based on these same calculations, the weight of the whole internet—every website, video, photo, emoji, and cat meme—is roughly 50 grams. By way of comparison, this is equivalent to the weight of a strawberry.

Weight alone does not determine significance or realness. Yet despite the relative weightlessness of digital media, they nevertheless place an incredible weight on us. It is amazing how something so weightless has become such a heavy weight in our lives and in our world.

It is very easy to use digital media in vapid ways such as for personal elevation, obsessively gazing at our own photos, posting praise for ourselves, or building our platform for personal gain. These are all forms of worshiping self, curving inward instead of outward. Yet we can find alternative ways to use digital media.

Let's examine two ways that we can begin to add more substance to digital media. A substantial and weightier use of digital media extends others, not just ourselves. Rather than using digital media as a narcissistic extension of ourselves, we can use digital media to extend Jesus and others. These are powerful ways to resist digital narcissism.

The Increase of Christ

While it is contrary to the world's way of doing things, digital media can and should extend the Gospel of Christ, rather than seeking our own glory. God alone is worthy of glory and praise: "Not to us, O LORD, not to us, but to Your name give glory, for the sake of Your steadfast love and Your faithfulness!" (Psalm 115:1).

John the Baptist declared, "He must increase, but I must

decrease" (John 3:30). As we interact with digital media, the followers of Jesus need to keep these words at the forefront of all our interactions. Before you snap, post, or tweet, ask yourself: Is this about me increasing or Christ increasing? This does not mean that each email, text, and post has to include a Bible verse. However, this question does insert a helpful pause into our digital interactions and invites us to consider who is getting the glory and praise.

The apostle Paul provides us with an example of using media for the increase of Christ. While Paul's media usage was neither digital nor print—he would have handwritten or dictated his epistles—he used media to communicate the Gospel of Jesus. In 2 Timothy, Paul instructed Timothy as follows: "When you come, bring the cloak that I left with Carpus at Troas, also the books, and above all the parchments" (2 Timothy 4:13). This verse makes it clear that Paul used media and wanted media. It is possible that Paul even loved media, since words and writing occupied so much of his life. Nevertheless, Paul did not use media in a narcissistic way. For Paul, the media he used were not aimed at his increase or glory. He used media in a way that caused himself to decrease and Christ to increase: "The saying is trustworthy and deserving of full acceptance, that Christ Jesus came into the world to save sinners, of whom I am the foremost" (1 Timothy 1:15).

The Increase of Others

It is so easy to use our social media channels to brag about ourselves, boast of our accomplishments, and bombard others with our awesomeness. Many of our digital interactions are treated as a zero-sum game: if we recognize the victories of others, then we must be the losers. This is simply not true. God invites and empowers us to put others before ourselves: "Do nothing from selfish ambition or conceit, but in humility count others more significant than yourselves. Let each of you look not only to his own interests, but also to the interests of others" (Philippians 2:3–4). Similarly, Romans 12 describes the Christian life as being aimed at the increase of others: "Love one another with brotherly affection. Outdo one another in showing honor. . . . Rejoice with those who rejoice, weep with those who weep" (verses 10, 15). Consider how these words of Scripture apply to our digital media interactions. In what ways do our comments show affection and honor to others? Do we ever stop to weep or pray when we encounter a hurting person online? Are our text messages humble or humblebrags, helpful to others or helpful to ourselves?

Not only is this biblical, it's also medical. Evidence shows that mental health may improve with less focus on oneself and more on others. Self-absorption, whether overly critical of oneself (as in mood and anxiety disturbance) or in love with oneself (as in narcissism), can be toxic. Therefore, some therapies give patients tools to reduce this self-absorption. One therapeutic approach called *mindfulness* works to get patients out of their own heads, breaking inward self-focus to focus awareness instead on the present moment and immediate surroundings. Self-absorption is a type of tunnel vision that makes one blind to the existence of others, the world, and God. It's no surprise then that self-centeredness and loneliness are mutually reinforcing. On the other hand, charitable, altruistic giving, when one provides for others in need without self-interest, may improve mood and even, paradoxically, one's self-esteem.

CONCLUSION

Digital narcissism is one of the unique temptations and traps of social media. In an effort to feel good about ourselves, we only succeed in becoming more miserable. Our maladaptive use of digital technology makes us distantly present during life's moments, destroys our common sense, numbs our senses and sense of self, and absorbs us in the self, when the true path to happiness and fulfillment lies beyond ourselves and in God. Digital technology is fleeting and illusory; God is real and enduring. Live for the eternal, not the temporary. Resist digital narcissism so that God is at the center of the universe, not yourself.

DISCUSSION QUESTIONS

1. What is narcissism?

2. How does digital technology feed into narcissism?

3. How is digital narcissism present in your life? Provide at least one specific example.

4. What steps can you take to resist digital narcissism? Consider how this may be accomplished through the increase of Christ and the increase of others.

DO THIS, NOT THAT

CALL-OUT CULTURE

Shakespeare added hundreds—some say even thousands—of words to the English language. The brilliant bard, however, has nothing on the panoply of new words generated by internet culture. The internet is constantly pumping out new words, jargon, and phrases.

Two of these newly coined internet expressions—*cancel culture* and *call-out culture*—have become especially popular. While cancel culture and call-out culture share some similarities, they are not identical.

Cancel culture aims to shut someone down as a way to punish an individual publicly for saying or doing something that is allegedly distasteful, hateful, or obtuse. People demand that the individual be "canceled"—removed from a concert lineup, dropped from a show or public appearance, or taken off bookshelves. Additionally, cancel culture may take the shape of finding photos on the internet from a march or rally, identifying specific individuals, and then contacting the person's employer demanding that the person be fired for attending the event.

Call-out culture, on the other hand, seeks to shame or call out an individual or organization publicly on social media for allegedly doing something wrong. To call someone out on social media is not necessarily demanding that someone be canceled or boycotted; rather, the aim is to let the whole world know that this individual is problematic. Call-out culture seeks to tear a person down by publicly calling the person out.

Certainly, at times people need to be held accountable for their words and actions—especially those that inflict harm on others. Nevertheless, both cancel culture and call-out culture are ripe for narcissism. At the very least, these can be fraught with hypocrisy. For example, Jesus said:

> Why do you see the speck that is in your brother's eye, but do not notice the log that is in your own eye? Or how can you say to your brother, "Let me take the speck out of your eye," when there is the log in your own eye? You hypocrite, first take the log out of your own eye, and then you will see clearly to take the speck out of your brother's eye. (Matthew 7:3–5)

Jesus also gave guidance for dealing with situations when someone is blatantly and repeatedly sinning (Matthew 18:15–20). It can certainly be appropriate for brothers and sisters in Christ to confront sin with the aim of repentance, forgiveness, and holiness.

However, the Bible does not talk only about calling out sins. God's Word has much to say about calling out one another *with encouragement*. Rather than exerting our efforts to publicly call out the faults of others, what about publicly calling out their virtues? Several Bible verses invite us to do this:

- Therefore encourage one another and build one another up, just as you are doing. (1 Thessalonians 5:11)

- Let no corrupting talk come out of your mouths, but only such as is good for building up, as fits the occasion, that it may give grace to those who hear. (Ephesians 4:29)

- Be kind to one another, tenderhearted, forgiving one another, as God in Christ forgave you. (Ephesians 4:32)

- And let us consider how to stir up one another to love and good works. (Hebrews 10:24)

As you use digital media, consider ways that you might use it to encourage others. How could you call out others—directly and discreetly or broadly and publicly—with words that build up and stir up one another to love and good works? Look for instances of someone doing something right, and let the world know. The internet has more than enough posts and articles about who is doing what wrong. Spurred on by the Word of God, the followers of Jesus can introduce the world to a better sort of call-out culture: calling out one another with kind, good, and encouraging words.

CHAPTER 7

WHEN COMPUTERS THINK FOR US

Victor Frankenstein and Garry Kasparov have little in common. Frankenstein is the fictional doctor in Mary Shelley's novel *Frankenstein*, while Kasparov is a real person born in 1963. Frankenstein came from Western Europe, studied chemistry, and worked as a scientist. Kasparov came from Eastern Europe, studied chess, and is a chess grandmaster.

Only one common thread ties these two men together: both men battled against laboratory creations.

Frankenstein created a sapient humanoid in his laboratory. It is unclear precisely how Frankenstein went about making this creature; some unknown combination of chemistry and alchemy resulted in a hideous, eight-foot-tall, fully feeling monster. Although not exactly human, this creation could think and act in ways that resembled a human. Through a series of clashes, Frankenstein battled against—and ultimately was bested by—this nonhuman opponent. After his creation murdered several of Frankenstein's loved ones, Frankenstein tracked the monster all the way to the North Pole and died of hypothermia while pursuing it.

Kasparov, on the other hand, did not create his nonhuman opponent. IBM did. A supercomputer called Deep Blue battled against Kasparov in a series of chess matches starting in 1996. Before competing against this machine, Kasparov had bested countless human opponents to become the youngest-ever chess World Champion in 1985. After proving his ability over human opponents, Kasparov began playing chess against computers. In 1985, the same year he became a world champion, Kasparov beat thirty-two chess computers. Then in 1996, Kasparov faced the IBM supercomputer known as Deep Blue. Kasparov won the initial six-game match in 1996. The computer won the next six-game match the year after, making this the first time that a computer had bested a world chess champion.

Both Frankenstein and Kasparov battled against laboratory creations. Both men were ultimately bested by their nonhuman opponents. Another well-known tale of man versus machine is that of John Henry. According to this American folktale, Henry bested the machine in a steel-driving competition against a steam drill. However, immediately after the competition ended, John Henry died, his heart bursting of exhaustion from the effort it took to triumph over the machine. It would seem that even when humans win against machines, the nonhuman opponents still come out victorious in the end.

HUMAN VS. MACHINE

When Kasparov lost to Deep Blue, some long-standing fears of humanity became a reality. Stretching far back into antiquity, humans have feared that their creations might one day surpass them—with dreadful consequences. Socrates mentioned how the statues made by the mythical craftsman Daedalus might one day become alive and walk off their pedestals. (Anyone who has ever seen the "Weeping Angels" episode from *Doctor Who* has had nightmares about this.)

FIGURE 6. Wagner and Mephistopheles watching the Homunculus. Illustration by Franz Xaver Steifensand for *Goethe's Works*, vol. 12 (Stuttgart and Tubingen: J. G. Cotta'sche Verlag, 1840), https://commons.wikimedia.org/wiki/File:%22FAUST._II.THEIL%E2%80%9D.jpg.

Johann Wolfgang von Goethe's *Faust* describes how a scientist named Wagner created a small, intelligent creature known as the Homunculus. As Wagner brings forth this being in a bottle, the devil—Mephistopheles—looks on with gleeful anticipation. Wagner describes this act of creating artificial intelligence as he declares:

It mounts, it glows, and doth together run,
One moment, and the work is done!
As mad, a grand design at first is view'd;
But we henceforth may laugh at fate,
And so a brain, with thinking-power embued,
Henceforth your living thinker will create.[39]

It is no coincidence that this brain-in-a-bottle Homunculus is created in the presence of the devil. While this creature does not end up being particularly monstrous, it is created in a laboratory teeming with prideful pursuit.

Mary Shelley's *Frankenstein*, as previously mentioned, depicts the creation of a sapient creature. This artificially intelligent and articulate creature admits that he is indeed fallen and evil: "Remember, that I am thy creature; I ought to be thy Adam; but I am rather the fallen angel, whom thou drivest from joy for no misdeed."[40] Unlike Narcissus, Frankenstein's creature stands over a pool of water, beholds his own image, and is revulsed by his hideous appearance. Shelley's depiction of this creature further perpetuated interest in and concern about artificial intelligence.

---

39 Johann von Goethe, *The Tragedy of Faust*, trans. Anna Swanwick, Part II, Act 2, in *The German Classics of The Nineteenth and Twentieth Centuries*, volume I, Masterpieces of German Literature Translated into English, in Twenty Volumes, Project Gutenberg, February 17, 2004, http://www.gutenberg.org/cache/epub/11123/pg11123-images.html.

40 Mary Shelley, *Frankenstein, Or, The Modern Prometheus*, Project Gutenberg, March 13, 2013, https://www.gutenberg.org/files/42324/42324-h/42324-h.htm.

A long history of concern surrounds artificially intelligent creations either surpassing or subjugating humans. Despite the concern over how and when human creations might one day surpass humanity, these concerns have been rather slow to materialize.

For example, in 1957, the Nobel-Prize-winning scholar Herbert Simon predicted that within a decade computers could beat humans in a game of chess. Simon believed that the computers of 1967 would be so sophisticated that they could beat human opponents. Forty years later, this prediction finally came true when IBM's Deep Blue beat Kasparov.

Contrary to the concerns of Goethe and Shelley, the world is not yet overrun by sapient creatures and artificially intelligent beings. Nevertheless, in the present age, computers and machines are increasingly overtaking human thinking. It is difficult to go a full day without having some created object—a website, a vehicle, or a computer—think for us.

LETTING COMPUTERS THINK FOR US

Artificial intelligence (AI) sounds futuristic. The term conjures thoughts of the Jetsons and Star Trek. But the term *artificial intelligence* is old enough to be collecting Social Security payments. AI, machines capable of performing a task that would otherwise require human intelligence, began in earnest in 1956. Emerging within the field of computer science, AI became a reality as a result of a conference known as the Dartmouth Workshop. At this symposium, computer scientists discussed how human intelligence might be performed by machines. John McCarthy, an attendee at the gathering, argued that the emerging field of research should be known as "artificial intelligence."

Broadly speaking, the two different categories of AI are

strong AI and weak AI. Strong AI, presently a theoretical concept, is a machine capable of wide-ranging intelligence such as commonsense knowledge, detailed reasoning, unguided learning, natural language communication, and planning. Also known as *artificial general intelligence*, this form of AI would closely resemble human intelligence. Strong AI is often depicted in science-fiction books and films—usually with a tragic or dystopian bent. While this sort of AI technology does not presently exist, technologists are working to turn this concept into a reality.

Weak AI is already a reality of daily life. This form of AI is ubiquitous: Siri, Alexa, Google, and Bing are all examples of weak AI. When a computer or machine is capable of performing a narrowly defined intelligent task, then it is considered weak AI.

Examples of weak AI include virtual assistants such as Siri and Alexa; these forms of AI are extremely knowledgeable when it comes to listening for voice commands and searching predefined databases. Yet these machines cannot accomplish anything outside the bounds of the engineered capabilities. Alexa can look up the price of a publicly traded stock, but she cannot work through the various reasons why it would be a good addition to your investment portfolio. Weak AI is a like a savant: highly proficient in a narrow field yet incapable elsewhere.

Countless forms of weak AI are all around us. Predictive text, the words suggested by your smartphone or computer, is weak AI. As you type a text message or email, the computer draws upon its knowledge of language and sentence structure. In this way, the machine is thinking for you as it proposes a way to complete your thought. Customer service chat bots, speechto-text tools, banking apps, and features on some vehicles are all examples of AI that we encounter on a daily basis.

Not surprisingly, AI abounds on the internet and social media. Search engines are driven by AI; every time you use Google or Bing, you are asking a computer to think for you. Similarly, fact-checking features on social media are at least partially automated by AI technology. When an article or news report is marked as misinformation, a computer may have made this determination. Similarly, when an internet search offers a nugget of information, a computer has performed this seemingly human act of intelligence.

So what if computers are thinking for us? Is it not to our benefit that we can ask a machine some of life's most important and deeply philosophical questions, such as "Why are clowns so scary?" or "Is my cat depressed?" It's kind of nice to have Siri and Alexa at your beck and call.

All kidding aside, AI offers many potential positives. Machine learning, a computer's ability to expand its knowledge without human intervention, could be a powerful force for good. Diagnosing diseases, recognizing fraudulent activity, and predicting catastrophic events are some of the benefits that can come from machine learning. To be sure, it is not entirely bad to have computers thinking for us.

Caution must complement any usage of AI. While the AI technology itself may not be all that problematic, the way that it is subtly transforming individuals and society as a whole can be hugely problematic. Jacques Ellul, a French sociologist and lay theologian, offers some important warnings in his influential book *The Technological Society*.

According to Ellul, technique is the one best way to perform a task or accomplish an outcome. For example, math teachers may teach students a technique for performing long division. This technique is the one best way to go about solving this math problem. Technique always strives toward greater productivity and improved efficiency in output.

Machines and technology, while different from technique, are closely related to it. Machines and technology are driven by pure technique; a computer calculator uses the one best way to solve a math problem. It is not as if your computer uses one technique to solve one math problem, then uses another technique to solve the next problem, and yet another technique to solve a third problem. Rather, one single and best technique is used every single time by the computer to produce the most efficient output.

While this may not seem immediately problematic, it can easily become a massive problem within society. By uncritically accepting the mindset of technique, the values of efficiency, productivity, and the pursuit of the single best way can soon become the sole factor in decision making and life in general.

- How do I finish this sentence? The computer knows the one best way to do so.

- What movie should I watch next? The computer knows my preferences better than I do.

- Who might make for a good spouse? Answer these questions, and the computer can figure that out with greater precision than you can.

- What should I believe? The fact-checking program knows.

- Does God exist? The computer can tell you. (By the way, this has actually happened. In 2013, two

143

computer scientists—Christoph Benzmüller of Berlin Free University and Bruno Woltzenlogel Paleo of the Technical University in Vienna—used an Apple MacBook to verify the twentieth-century mathematician Kurt Gödel's logical proof of God's existence. Gödel's proof of God's existence was based upon the work of Anselm of Canterbury in the late eleventh century.)

When computers think for us, we lose freedom, creativity, and diversity. Why think for yourself when the computer has already determined the best way? Why use your own brain to finish a sentence, find some information, or make a decision when it has already been handed to you? Why should people in India or Greenland live differently if the computer knows the one best way to accomplish the outcomes of business or education?

An example of a situation in which this overreliance on machines has the potential for harm is in the training of student doctors in preparation for their future practice of medicine. Having a world of medical facts at our fingertips can lead us to believe that we're experts. As Dr. Smith knows firsthand, this easy access changes the role of teachers in medical education. Teachers are no longer needed for the facts, but they should not be dismissed from the educational process. Teachers have a role; it's just changed. Teachers help medical students learn how to evaluate and apply information critically.

An extremely wide range exists when it comes to the quality of information through electronic media. Some medical information on the internet is blatantly false (surprise, surprise!) and dangerous. Other medical information has a strong evidence base and is reputable. Sorting through this information and understanding how to apply it properly to the right situation takes experience. There is no shortcut to becoming an expert. When students experience a false sense of competence because of electronic knowledge (what those in medicine sometimes call "peripheral brains") and rush to treat real people, mistakes happen. As credited to Alexander Pope, "A little learning is a dangerous thing." A personal sense of omniscience, knowing everything, is always false; only God knows everything. Humanity's attempts to create a machine as impressive as the human mind have always fallen short.

When it comes to medicine, nothing can substitute for the human brain, and we do not want to be helpless if the power goes out and technology fails. For doctors to serve people best, they need to have knowledge in their own brains and have practiced critical thinking sufficiently so that function exists within their own skulls. Most medical students have still-developing brains—human brains are not fully developed until the mid to late twenties—and allowing computers to do too much thinking for us can lead to a loss of critical ways of thinking for ourselves.

According to Ellul, technique worships nothing and can easily become a god unto itself. Since everything has to answer to the one best way of technique, it seeks to be the sole arbiter of knowledge. Ellul warns that technique and technology can become objects for worship when humans fear, love, and trust in technique above all else.

Furthermore, it is unlikely that technique and technology such as AI will always be aimed in the right direction. AI can tell you the one best way—the most productive way—to invest in profitable stocks and make lots of money; however, this gain may come at the cost of others falling into poverty. AI can tell you which candidate is the one best person for a job, and yet it may also have racial or socioeconomic biases built into its computer coding. AI may lead to the one best way to cure a disease; still, access to this treatment may be narrowly available to the wealthy and powerful. If efficiency and technique are the only values considered in a decision, other values get lost in the process, often to the harm of the people around us.

Martin Luther, though living long before computers and AI technology, offers wisdom for using these powerful tools:

> Just look at your tools—at your needle or thimble, your beer barrel, your goods, your scales or yard-stick or measure. . . . All this is continually crying out to you: "Friend, use me in your relations with your neighbor just as you would want your neigh-bor to use his property in his relations with you."[41]

Although computers may be able to think for us, we must guard against using these tools in ways that hurt our neighbors and society.

LETTING OTHERS THINK FOR US

We often rely on outside sources, especially electronic, for our information. How do we know what is false and what is true? Everyone has an opinion, and you can find plenty on the internet. However, not all opinions are equal. Not all opinions are supported by facts. Media literacy, the ability to access and evaluate media critically, is a valuable skill. Computer algorithms often present us with biased information, essentially editing what we see according to a specific agenda (whether created by the company whose product we are using or generated by our own patterns of internet use). This edited version of life often

---

41 LW 21:237.

misses the nuances of the real world's three-dimensional people and complex issues.

Often, computers present us with digital media that it thinks we will like. Sometimes computers present us with content that will provoke our fear and anger. There may be an agenda behind this information with the intent to cause us to behave in a certain way. Being exposed to online information first impacts our thoughts, then it changes our behaviors. As discussed in chapter 3, behavioral contagion is at work here (more on this in chapter 9). When we are exposed to someone else demonstrating a behavior, we may mimic that behavior, especially if we strongly identify with that person or group. Seeing a social media post about an outraged friend or role model may incite you to mimic their behavior and become outraged as well.

This influence can affect us deeply, even if we don't realize it. Paul McClure, sociology professor at the University of Lynchburg, has done extensive research on how religious belief is influenced by others via the internet and social media. McClure found that using social networking sites correlates with increased acceptance of religious syncretism (that is, mixing beliefs from various religious traditions). People who use social networking sites are more likely to be open to the notion of picking and choosing one's religious beliefs from a variety of different traditions.[42]

McClure's research findings also indicate that social media use inclines people toward "spiritual tinkering" and religiously eclectic beliefs, even when it is contrary to what their religious tradition teaches. For example, a person may religiously identify with the Christian tradition but, through the influence of

---

42 Paul K. McClure, "Faith and Facebook in a Pluralistic Age: The Effects of Social Networking Sites on the Religious Beliefs of Emerging Adults," *Sociological Perspectives* 59, no. 4 (Winter 2016): 818–34, https://doi.org/10.1177%2F0731121416647361.

extensive social media use, may adopt notions of karma and reincarnation from Eastern religions.

This tendency toward spiritual tinkering or religious bricolage is the result not only of the technology but also of the social interaction that happens through technology. McClure suggests that the changes to one's religious thinking occur through the ongoing interaction with others online. That is to say, other people play a part in how we formulate our religious beliefs. We look to what others are doing in their lives and allow that to change our own—essentially, letting others think for us.

These research findings echo the words of Scripture:

> Take care lest you forget the LORD, who brought you out of the land of Egypt, out of the house of slavery. It is the LORD your God you shall fear. Him you shall serve and by His name you shall swear. You shall not go after other gods, the gods of the peoples who are around you. (Deuteronomy 6:12–14)

Israel was constantly tempted by the prospect of looking to other people for help in constructing their beliefs and spiritual practices. Not unlike how people today look to the religious beliefs of others on the internet and social media, ancient Israel looked to the Canaanites, Moabites, and Philistines. Letting others think for us is not a new problem. But it is a problem—especially when it comes to our religious beliefs.

The internet and social media are not the only places where technology invites others to think for us. Self-driving vehicles, fully autonomous vehicles in which a passenger does nothing while being transported from one place to another, are a prime example of how technology allows others to think for us. Countless decisions—how fast to accelerate and brake, the speed at which turns are taken, and what to do in emergency situations—are predetermined in autonomous vehicles. What to do if this light turns yellow? Is the safest action to stop, swerve, or accelerate? In an autonomous vehicle, someone else makes these decisions ahead of time. Engineers, computer programmers, and companies make crucial decisions and then write these decisions into the vehicle's computer coding.

What should be done if a pedestrian suddenly walks in front of an autonomous vehicle? Is it best to spare the life of the passenger in the vehicle while killing the person outside the vehicle? Or should it be the other way around? In an effort to have others think for us, researchers from the Massachusetts Institute of Technology have created a website called "Moral Machine." This website presents various difficult decisions that might arise with autonomous vehicles so that people can think through the situation and offer what they think is the most moral action to take. These responses will then be translated into the computer coding of autonomous vehicles, resulting in a sort of morality by majority.

Whether scrolling through Twitter, researching a topic on Wikipedia, or traveling in an autonomous vehicle, technology presents us with the serious predicament of others thinking for us.

WHEN WE THINK FOR OURSELVES

It is problematic when we stop thinking and computers think for us. It is also problematic when we stop thinking and let others think for us. So, then, we ought to think for ourselves. We should throw off the shackles of both computers and the community and think only for ourselves. Rather than seeking answers from computers or other people, we should look within to find the answers. Right?

Not exactly.

Thinking for ourselves—that is, looking within ourselves for truth, wisdom, and certainty—can be just as problematic as looking to AI technology or the internet hive mind. In reality, looking within and thinking for ourselves is not a viable way forward.

Trevin Wax, in his book *Rethink Your Self: The Power of Looking Up before Looking In*, points out how conventional wisdom tells us to look within ourselves first, then to look at the people around us, and lastly to look to God. If ever we are lost, confused, scared, or unsure what we should believe, we wrongly think that the best place to look is inside of ourselves. Wax uses a litany of common expressions to demonstrate how this is a widely held view: You do you. Be true to yourself. Follow your heart. Chase your dreams.

But are we sure that what is within us is entirely reliable and trustworthy? God's Word should cause us to second-guess this approach. Jesus did not tell people to look within to find sure and certain truths. Listen to what Jesus said to a crowd of people in Matthew 15:

> It is not what goes into the mouth that defiles a
> person, but what comes out of the mouth; this de-
> files a person. . . . But what comes out of the mouth
> proceeds from the heart, and this defiles a person.
> For out of the heart come evil thoughts, murder,
> adultery, sexual immorality, theft, false witness,
> slander. These are what defile a person. (Matthew
> 15:11, 18–20)

Jesus bluntly states that looking within ourselves will yield evil thoughts, lies, greed, and confusion. Paul echoes this same point in Romans 7:18–20:

> For I know that nothing good dwells in me, that is, in my flesh. For I have the desire to do what is right, but not the ability to carry it out. For I do not do the good I want, but the evil I do not want is what I keep on doing. Now if I do what I do not want, it is no longer I who do it, but sin that dwells within me.

Looking within ourselves for certainty often leads to the wrong conclusions. Your brain can lie to you. These kinds of irrational thoughts and beliefs are called *cognitive distortions*, and we unknowingly strengthen them over time.

One example of a cognitive distortion is overgeneralization, in which we take one example and generalize it. For instance, "A French exchange student stole my girlfriend at summer camp. He was an arrogant jerk. All French men are rude and pompous." We are also more prone to cognitive errors when we think while we are emotional—hot cognition. When we are calm, we realize that it is never a good choice to escalate a road rage situation. But this feels a lot different when we are behind the wheel of a car and someone has just cut us off in traffic and flashed a middle finger. What makes these cognitive distortions even trickier to control is that we most often have no conscious awareness of them. One example is *implicit bias*, a term that describes unconscious stereotypical thoughts about people different from us, influencing our attitudes and behaviors.

Scripture makes it clear: Looking in is no better than looking out. So where do we turn? If computers, others, and ourselves all fail us, where do we look to find a knowledge that is sure and certain, trustworthy and enduring?

GOD'S THINKING FOR YOU

Knowledge that is sure and certain, trustworthy and enduring is found in Jesus: "If you abide in My word, you are truly My disciples, and you will know the truth, and the truth will set you free" (John 8:31–32). The word of Jesus is truth. The center of our thinking, knowledge, wisdom, and truth is not generated by computers, crowd-sourced online, or found within. It is only found in Jesus, the way, the truth, and the life.

In John 17, what is known as the High Priestly Prayer, we hear Jesus praying to God the Father:

> I have given them Your word, and the world has hated them because they are not of the world, just as I am not of the world. I do not ask that You take them out of the world, but that You keep them from the evil one. They are not of the world, just as I am not of the world. Sanctify them in the truth; Your word is truth. As You sent Me into the world, so I have sent them into the world. And for their sake I consecrate Myself, that they also may be sanctified in truth. (verses 14–19)

Notice what Jesus says—the Word of God is truth. The people of God have been sent into the world with the truth. God's Word is not some esoteric, out-of-touch, ethereal wisdom. It is truth for life in this world.

God's Word is often referred to as the norm that norms. That is to say, God's Word is the thing that determines the basis of reality and our beliefs. We need not look online or within to find the truth. As the Book of Proverbs says, "Trust in the LORD with all your heart, and do not lean on your own understanding. In all your ways acknowledge Him, and He will make straight your paths" (3:5–6).

The mind of God is revealed in the Word of God by the Holy Spirit (1 Corinthians 2:6–16). Scripture is God's thinking for you. God speaks words of love for you. God speaks words of mercy for you. God speaks words of wisdom for you. This Word is eternal, enduring, and true. And it is a Word for you.

Oswald Bayer can help us understand the significance of how God's Word is for you.[43] According to Bayer, the language of "for you" highlights the giver more than the receiver. It is the giver who determines that something is given for you. Nevertheless, God's Word being given for you implies a human recipient. Something that is given is also received. When we hear and believe that God's Word has been given "for you," we receive God's gifts given in love to His creatures.

With God's thinking for you at the center, other ways of thinking can find their proper place. The Word of God adjudicates all that we encounter through computers and artificial intelligence, in other people, and inside of us. The Word of God judges the thinking that happens by way of technology, deeming it to be right or wrong, good or bad, wise or foolish.

The psalmist declares, "Make me to know Your ways, O LORD; teach me Your paths. Lead me in Your truth and teach me, for You are the God of my salvation; for You I wait all the day long" (25:4–5). Led by the Lord along His paths, we walk the one best way. While some may fear the possibility of artificial intelligence surpassing or subjecting humanity, the people

---

43 Oswald Bayer, "The Self-Giving God," *Lutheran Quarterly* 33, no. 2 (Summer 2019): 125–36.

of God know that "if God is for us, who can be against us?" (Romans 8:31).

CONCLUSION

Humans have a complicated relationship with intelligent machines—especially when we rely on these machines to think for us. While we initially create these machines, they have the power to change us, and not always for the better. We must navigate the pitfalls of having others, including machines, doing the thinking for us. However, the solution is not to do all of the thinking ourselves, searching for knowledge within. The Word of God is the ultimate source of knowledge that is sure and certain, trustworthy and enduring. When we rely first and foremost on God's thinking for us as the core of our mental processes, He leads us in the truth.

DISCUSSION QUESTIONS

1. Describe situations in which computers think for you in your daily life.

2. How dependent are you on digital technology to function? How does it impact your life when you lose access to digital technology?

3. What are the pitfalls of having others think for us? Describe how you will more critically review the media you consume.

4. How does thinking for yourself compare to God's thinking for you?

DO THIS, NOT THAT

EMBRACE INEFFICIENCY

Wendell Berry, in his poem "Manifesto: The Mad Farmer Liberation Front," invites his hearers to "do something that won't compute." Modern life is increasingly driven by technique and the pursuit of the one best way. Doing something that won't compute means doing something unproductive or inefficient.

Sabbath rest subverts the world of production, efficiency, and technique. God describes the Sabbath as follows:

Six days you shall labor and do all your work, but the seventh day is a Sabbath to the LORD your God. On it you shall not do any work, you or your son or your daughter or your male servant or your female servant, or your ox or your donkey or any of your livestock, or the sojourner who is within your gates, that your male servant and your female servant may rest as well as you. You shall remember that you were a slave in the land of Egypt, and the LORD your God brought you out from there with a mighty hand and an outstretched arm. Therefore the LORD your God commanded you to keep the Sabbath day. (Deuteronomy 5:13–15)

Taking a day off after six days of work may not seem all that revolutionary or subversive. However, there's more going on here.

Sabbath rest involves trust. By telling His people to take a day off from working, God invites us into a relationship of

trust. If you are not working, then you are not being productive or efficient. Your inbox is not being tended and your
to-do list is not being checked off. This is where trust comes
in—taking time off for Sabbath rest means trusting that God
will provide even in our resting. Shutting the computers down
and spending time in worship is an act of trust in God. You are
trusting that He will provide even when you are not working.
You are trusting that time in worship is time well spent, even if
it is not productive or efficient by the world's standards.

Sabbath rest involves others. God did not draw the
bounds of Sabbath rest narrowly. It is not as if only the people of Israel were invited to a life marked by Sabbath rest, but
the rest of their workers and livestock had to work all day and
every day. Although it was not productive or efficient, God
included everyone when it came to establishing the bounds of
Sabbath rest: children, servants, sojourners, and livestock. This
would have involved lost wages (or at least a loss of potential
income) for the people of Israel. On a spreadsheet, this decision did not compute. And yet God invited Israel to remember
when they were slaves in Egypt and to consider how He merci-
fully delivered them from bondage.

Sabbath rest involves worship. In this chapter, we explored the topic of God's thinking for you. Rather than relying
on computers, other people, or even our own thinking, we
rely on God's thinking for us. Worship is part of Sabbath rest.
Worship relies on God—His Word, His presence, His gifts—and
it is where we meet God through His Word and Sacraments.
In worship, God gratuitously pours out good gifts to you and
for you; you can find rest in receiving the bounty of God's love
and generosity. Worship is an encounter with God's Word

for you. Worship is a feast of God's mercy for you. Worship is God's work of salvation prepared and presented for you.

In its ancient context, Sabbath rest did not compute. The thought of giving slaves, servants, and sojourners a day of rest would be the height of inefficiency. In our modern context, Sabbath rest still does not compute. A day free from emails, spreadsheets, to-do lists, and accomplishing tasks is not the best way to be productive. Yet it is the only way to trust in God and God alone. Sabbath rest is not efficient or productive. Sabbath rest does not compute. And that's the point.

CHAPTER 8

BEAUTY AND BLINDNESS IN A DIGITAL AGE

Graffiti is a visual nuisance. It is illegal in many places to spray paint on cement walls, train cars, and public buildings. The rationale behind these laws is fairly simple: public spaces should not be spoiled by someone spray-painting a message for all to see.

However, the street artist Banksy has helped the world to see graffiti as art. Although his true identity is unknown, Banksy is known throughout the world for his iconic works of public art. For good or for ill, many people today can more readily identify a Banksy than a Bruegel or a Bernini.

Banksy's artwork is memorable largely because of *where* it appears—public spaces, alleyways, subway depots, and cement walls. For example, many of Banksy's works appear on the separation wall dividing Israel and Palestine. Spray-painted onto this politically charged wall are depictions of young children walking through a hole in the cement barrier. Others depict a little girl floating over the wall while holding onto a bunch of balloons or a man pulling the wall apart like a curtain to reveal a beautiful beach on the other side. Nearby, in Bethlehem, Banksy has painted satirical works depicting a donkey undergoing a security check by a soldier, a rioter throwing a bundle of flowers, and a girl reaching for a heart-shaped balloon.

Rupturing the tense mood of the West Bank, these works of public art capture the attention of nearly anyone passing by. Amid the violence of the region, these spray-painted creations are instances of beauty that are out of place. With radiant color and startling messages in otherwise bleak spaces, Banksy's works are visually dissonant and arresting. These works force you to *see* again.

BANKRUPT ON BEAUTY

Beauty has been bankrupted by digital media. A torrent of distorted digital images on the internet and social media have left us blind to the beauty of the world around us. Billions of pixels have blinded us to authentic beauty. The ability to edit, filter, and adjust photographs has flooded our eyes with manipulated images of the human body. We are left with unrealistic expectations of how we ought to look and a low self-image when we cannot measure up to these manufactured images. Endless opportunities to watch videos, scroll through photos, and look at screens has left us largely unable to see authentic beauty all around us.

In this world of bankrupted beauty, we need to learn to see again. The world desperately needs the uniquely Christian ways of understanding beauty and seeing that which is beautiful. Just as Banksy's public art has helped people in the West Bank to see again, uniquely Christian understanding and approaches to beauty can help the world to see again.

THE BEAUTY OF THE CROSS

Christianity has a robust heritage of aesthetics, art, and

beauty. Many of humanity's greatest artistic works—paintings, sculptures, musical compositions, and literary works—were inspired by the Christian faith. However, recent generations of Christians have seemingly undervalued the role of beauty in the Christian faith. Beauty is often deemed unimportant or unnecessary as it relates to Christianity. This is a tragic development, since God's creation has truth, beauty, and goodness woven throughout it. And the central event of Christianity—the cross of Christ—is supremely beautiful.

To develop a Christian understanding of beauty, we must learn what it means for something to be beautiful. What is beauty? Is beauty merely in the eye of the beholder and subject to the whims of the viewer? Is beauty synonymous with sexual attraction or awe-inspiring grandeur?

As with all things, Christians turn to Scripture as the arbiter of truth in questions of beauty. Paul warned the Church in Corinth that the world's ways—wisdom, knowledge, truth—are often in conflict with God (1 Corinthians 1–2). Similarly, the world's pattern of beauty differs from divine patterns of beauty.

Biblically speaking, beauty is that which reflects God's reality (Psalm 27:4; 96:6). Conformity to the will of God, living in sync with God, is beautiful (1 Peter 3:4). In this sense, what appears to be ugly or distasteful to the world may be beautiful according to God (Matthew 26:10), and what the world calls beautiful may be ugly according to the standards of the kingdom of God (Matthew 23:27).

The cross is an example of God's peculiar beauty. Christ Jesus, according to the prophet Isaiah, was far from beautiful according to worldly standards: "For He grew up before Him like a young plant, and like a root out of dry ground; He had no form or majesty that we should look at Him, and no beauty that

161

we should desire Him" (Isaiah 53:2). Although Jesus is lacking beauty according to worldly standards, He exudes true beauty because His life conforms to the will of God.

Thus the cross is beautiful despite the blood and agony, wormwood and gall. The cross is the epicenter of God's beauty because that is where humanity finds love, life, and peace. The message of the cross and those who bear this message are beautiful (Romans 10:15). Although sin has marred God's beautiful creation with the ugliness of death, Jesus makes all things new, bright, and beautiful.

The modern theologian Jeremy Begbie, professor at Duke Divinity School, has also argued that any Christian understanding of beauty must be centered on Christ and the cross. According to Begbie, the incarnation of Jesus has fundamentally changed humanity and our relation to the physical world, including beauty: humanity has been incorporated into the Trinity by the Son of God. The Godhead has assumed human flesh in Christ Jesus. The Holy Spirit liberates us from our self-obsession and enables us to respond rightly to the created world.

But that's not the totality of God's beauty. Anchored in Christ Jesus and the cross as the core of divine beauty, Christians can make their lives beautiful by living in sync with God according to who He has made you to be. Beauty abounds in the created world. True beauty, that which reflects God's reality and conforms to the will of God, can be found in the most ordinary places: neighborhoods, churches, living rooms, forests, hospitals, classrooms, and elsewhere. Realizing that God's creation is beautiful—even in its uncropped, unfiltered, and unedited form—invites us both to delight in the created world and worship the One who made it all.

THE BEAUTY OF THE HUMAN BODY

God's Word makes it abundantly clear: the human body is beautiful. Since it was made by God, and since He continues daily and richly to provide for our bodies, the human body is full of beauty and wonder: "I praise You, for I am fearfully and wonderfully made. Wonderful are Your works; my soul knows it very well" (Psalm 139:14).

But as we know, God's standards of beauty aren't like the world's. To say that the human body is beautiful does not imply flawless skin or chiseled features. Rather, the human body is beautiful when it reflects God's reality and conforms to the will of God: "Or do you not know that your body is a temple of the Holy Spirit within you, whom you have from God? You are not your own, for you were bought with a price. So glorify God in your body" (1 Corinthians 6:19–20).

Our bodies are beautiful when they are used by God according to His beautiful plans and purposes:

> I appeal to you therefore, brothers, by the mercies of God, to present your bodies as a living sacrifice, holy and acceptable to God, which is your spiritual worship. Do not be conformed to this world, but be transformed by the renewal of your mind, that by testing you may discern what is the will of God, what is good and acceptable and perfect. (Romans 12:1–2)

The human body is loved and cherished by God. Even the words spoken as part of the Christian committal service testify to God's great love for the body:

> May God the Father, who created this body; may

God the Son, who by His blood redeemed this
body; may God the Holy Spirit, who by Holy Baptism sanctified this body to be His temple, keep
these remains to the day of the resurrection of all
flesh. Amen.[44]

God loves and cherishes our bodies—even without filters,
alterations, or makeup—so much that He would redeem them
with His blood and sanctify them by Holy Baptism and the in-
dwelling of the Holy Spirit. This is a powerful testimony to the
beauty of the human body.

However, the world loves to distort beauty, holding up
as beautiful things that are against God's definition. Pornography is an example of this so-called beauty: it celebrates using the body in ways that are plainly sinful and contrary to the
will of God. Pornography claims to be beautiful but is actually
hideous.

The way digital media portray human bodies is another
example. Many people struggle with some level of self-esteem
issues because of the world's filtered and distorted beauty standards. A more extreme example is body dysmorphic disorder,
a mental health condition that involves seeing flaws in one's appearance that do not exist or are greatly exaggerated. For example, a patient with a normal nose may believe that his or her
nose is horribly misshapen and hideously ugly. What we see in
the surrounding culture and in the black mirrors of our screens
influences how we see ourselves. Filters distort our images and
may lead to the false belief that our Snapchat images are our
true selves and that our real selves are flawed. This mismatch
between the real self in the mirror and the version in a digital
image can cause significant distress.

---

44 *Pastoral Care Companion* (St. Louis: Concordia Publishing House, 2007), 134.

In some cases, people undergo surgeries to look like their digital versions, blind to the beauty and worth they already have as God's creation. Extreme and repeated visual alterations can further damage self-esteem and cause distress, and structural alterations are often unsatisfying and irreversible. Although modern medicine and technology make it possible for us to do these sorts of things, this does not mean that we always should do them. We are not our own creators. Instead, we can learn to cherish the bodies we have been given just as God loves and cherishes them.

BLINDNESS IN A DIGITAL AGE

With these uniquely Christian understandings of beauty in place, we can turn to the topic of blindness in the digital age. The dizzying increase of digital noise in this modern age has left us in a peculiar paradox: we have more to see than ever before, yet we are seeing less and less of the world around us. Much of this has to do with the digital screens we hang on our walls, carry in our pockets, and stare at all day.

The earliest high-definition screens were available to consumers around the late 2000s. These screens had 1,080 pixels—tiny light-emitting valves—down the vertical face of the screen and 1,920 pixels in the other direction. Hence, they were referred to as 1080p screens. A decade later, around the mid-2010s, ultra-high-definition screens came out. These had significantly more pixels—3,840 by 2,160—and thus had a far sharper resolution. These were referred to as 4K.

As with all things technological, this was not enough. Around 2015, 8K resolution boasted a stunning 7,680 by 4,320 pixels. The trajectory of digital screens has been steadily moving toward more pixels, sharper resolution, and a more vivid viewing experience.

But something strange is happening. Despite all those pixels, blindness abounds. The visual glut of the digital age, with its 85-inch television screens, dazzling Instagram photos, and endless megapixels, has actually eroded our ability to see.

This is not a new concern. Well before 4K and 8K, a twentieth-century German philosopher named Josef Pieper was alarmed by the excess of visuals in the modern world. In his book *Only the Lover Sings*, Pieper discusses the concept of visual noise. Just as it is difficult to have a conversation in a loud space because of all the ambient noise, it is difficult to see in visually noisy spaces. Our capacity to see is diminished because there is simply so much to see. Pieper argued that rather than help us see and perceive more, television and screens blunt our ability to see. He wasn't suggesting that our physiological eyesight changes; rather, we begin to lose our ability to observe God's creation and perceive reality, both spiritually and physically.

Although he was a philosopher and not a physician, Pieper's observations can be understood medically as a form of sensory gating. Sensory gating is the neurological process through which our brains filter out unnecessary stimuli, all the noise. This process allows us to tune out the sound of a noisy fan in a room, for example. The sound fades to the background the longer we are exposed to it. However, when our brain is assaulted by a tidal wave of visual stimuli, our sensory gating system is overwhelmed and cannot perform this filtering function.

Years after Pieper made his arguments, researchers Christopher Chabris and Daniel Simons demonstrated a similar point. Chabris and Simons conducted the now well-known invisible gorilla experiment to show how visual noise can blind us.[45]

The experiment went like this: Participants were asked to watch a video of six people passing around basketballs. In the video, three people wore white shirts and three people wore black shirts. The participants in the experiment were asked to count the number of passes made by the people in the white shirts.

But then, halfway through the video, something strange happens: a gorilla walks into the middle of the frame, thumps its chest, and ambles away. Certainly, this strange sighting would be noticeable to all watching the video.

Nope.

When asked about the gorilla in the video, half of the people had completely missed seeing it. Half of the people watching the video did not see a gorilla enter the room. The visual noise and flurry of activity in the video caused the experiment participants to miss something as obvious and out of place as a gorilla thumping its chest.

Pieper's reflections on visual noise, along with the concept of sensory gating and the research findings of Chabris and Simons, should give us pause. Are we blinded by digital media? If so, what are we not seeing? What does it matter if the digital age is making us blind?

The stakes are higher than you might think. According to Pieper, the abundance of screens and digital media actually damages our spiritual capacity to perceive what is real, true, and beautiful. Pieper feared that once humans fell below a certain threshold of seeing, they would lose their ability to recognize any spiritual realities in this world. The visual noise of

---

45 Daniel J. Simons and Christopher F. Chabris, "Gorillas in Our Midst: Sustained Inattentional Blindness for Dynamic Events," *Perception* 28, no. 9 (September 1999): 1059–74, https://doi.org/10.1068%2Fp281059.

the digital age diverts our attention away from the wonder and beauty of God's creation all around us.

As we check our phone for the 231st time, we are bound to miss something truly beautiful: a hopeful sprig of grass sprouting, a plume of clouds drifting overhead, or a tiny ant heroically carrying a leaf in its jaw. The siren song of screens draws our eyes away from the simple beauty that God has afforded to sunshine, soil, and shadows. Our focus on the digital pixels of faces on social media inhibits our ability to see the real faces of people around us for whom Jesus lived and loved, died and rose again. Eternally meaningful realities can become invisible to us as a result of visual noise. In this visual age, we must consider the words of Psalm 119:37: "Turn my eyes from looking at worthless things; and give me life in Your ways."

The Hedonic Treadmill

How is it possible that humanity can make such advancements in visual technology yet become blind in the process? This may have something to do with the hedonic treadmill, the psychological process through which humans revert to their normal happiness threshold after major life changes. Changes in life, such as technological advancements, can raise the threshold for happiness, contentment, or satisfaction, but not for long.

For example, a thirty-inch color television is pleasurable. Upgrading to a forty-inch television seems better and more pleasurable. But this happiness only lasts until your psychological processes adjust to a stable set point. Before long, the pleasure of the forty-inch television is about the same as with the smaller television. Taking these steps toward a bigger and better television does not translate into significant progress in happiness, contentment, or satisfaction—hence the treadmill. Sometimes with intense, unnatural changes, such as substance use or extreme use of technology, this happiness threshold can be altered so that normal, natural life events no longer lead to feelings of happiness. In this case, only the drugs or the technology bring pleasure, however fleeting, and a cycle of addiction develops.

LEARNING TO SEE AGAIN

Learning to see again in a digital world is not easy, but it's not impossible. Josef Pieper did not merely diagnose the problem without also proposing a solution. Surprisingly, Pieper prescribes things such as leisure, Sabbath rest, and worship as the remedy for the blindness that is so common in the digital age.

In his book *Leisure: The Basis of Culture*, Pieper argues that modern life has become so focused on work and productivity that it has lost any concept of leisure. Ancient thinkers, such as Aristotle, argued that we should be unleisurely in order to have leisure—that is, we work only as much as we need to in order to have leisure.

But our modern society is completely focused on work and productivity. Because we are constantly busy, always on the move, perpetually seeking stimulation, and going a million miles an hour, we have no room for leisure. Pieper claims that the death of leisure sends ripples out into some unexpected places: society, education, art, and religion. In short, human flourishing fades, creativity ceases, and the God-given goodness of life languishes in a world without leisure.

What exactly is leisure, though? Is it kicking your feet up, snoozing on a hammock, or a day of low-key lounging in sweatpants? Not exactly. Leisure is related to worship. Throughout human history, feasts have been religiously oriented times of leisure. Festivals, which are a cause for feasting, abound in the Christian liturgical calendar. The festivals of Christmas, Easter, and Ascension are times of worship, Sabbath rest, and leisure.

Leisure is more than merely loafing around. Leisure is related to worship because the Divine Service is a time when we rest in God and receive from God. Martin Luther described this as the *vita passiva*, or passive life. Unlike the active life (*vita activa*) and the contemplative life (*vita contemplativa*), the *vita passiva* is not about doing but rather receiving. The *vita passiva* is a life of receptivity: receiving the gifts of Christ through the Holy Spirit, receiving God's Word and Sacraments, and being receptive to God's calling in our various vocations. This sort of leisure is vital for human flourishing and learning to see again.

Yet one might argue that binge-watching TV shows is a sort of *vita passiva*. Aren't I passively receiving something when I park myself on the couch for a few hours of streaming shows, playing video games, or scrolling through social media? While this may be a form of passive reception, consider what we are receiving: something fabricated, vapid, and fleeting. Made by someone else, relevant only for a time, and not meaningful in itself, these sorts of creations pale in comparison to God's eternally relevant gifts in worship. Centered on the heavenly beauty of the cross of Christ, worship is leisurely time spent in the presence of God's peculiar and eternal beauty.

Worship is the remedy for our frenetic pace and digitally induced blindness, but other habits can help us learn to see again too.

Visual or digital fasting, similar to fasting from food, can help us develop a greater sensitivity toward and appreciation for what we see. This could look like setting a period of the day or week to be screen-free, listening to music while going to sleep instead of watching television, or turning your phone or computer completely off for a day.

Looking at beautiful artwork is another way to help our digitally impaired vision. By either creating or viewing works of art, we must develop awareness and patient receptivity to what is not immediately apparent. Staring at a painting or sculpture for five or ten minutes can be agonizingly boring for people who are yet to be weaned from the visual noise of digital media. And yet these five or ten minutes of agony can reveal much that the eye had overlooked at first glance. Art helps us realize the old adage that there is often more than meets the eye.

A great example of this is the work of the surrealist painter René Magritte. One of Magritte's most famous works, *The Treachery of Images*, illustrates how a work of art can help us learn to see again. Magritte's painting shows an image of a pipe along with French text, *Ceci n'est pas une pipe* ("This is not a pipe"). At first glance, this painting appears inconsistent: what you see, despite the text claiming otherwise, is most certainly a pipe. Yet Magritte invites viewers to see and think more closely. The painting is not a pipe; it's an image of one. It is a visual representation of a pipe, not a pipe in reality. Magritte opens our eyes with this work of art and helps us learn to see again, similar to Banksy's works mentioned earlier.

Gazing upon the beauty of God's creation is another powerful way to recover beauty in this digital age. The psalmist declares, "One thing have I asked of the LORD, that will I seek after: that I may dwell in the house of the LORD all the days of my life, to gaze upon the beauty of the LORD and to inquire in His temple" (27:4). The beauty of the Lord is seen in worship as we encounter the peculiar beauty of the cross of Christ and receive the beautiful gift of God's Word and Sacraments. And yet the beauty of God bursts out beyond the house of the Lord and into every nook and cranny of His creation.

Spending time in God's creation can clear away the visual noise and open our eyes. Marvel at the delicate fiddleheads of a fern as they emerge and unroll. Linger over the swirls and bursts of water in a river. Be enchanted by snowflakes sweetly descending like manna from heaven. Stare at the nighttime sky long enough so that your pupils, cones, and rods can gain sensitivity to faint stars and fleeting meteors. God's glory is waiting to be seen! (And while doing these things, resist the impulse to pull out your phone and take a picture for Instagram.)

CONCLUSION

We are blinded by our own digital creations. In the process of being increasingly overwhelmed by visual stimuli, we have traded in real beauty for pixels and shortchanged ourselves. We bought the lie that more pixels lead to more happiness; we transformed our bodies on the internet, and sometimes in real life, into pixelated images. In order to learn to see again, we must spend less time pursuing distracting thoughts, images, and activities and more time in leisurely reception of the gifts of God in Christ Jesus. By turning down the visual noise, we can see true beauty: Christ, the cross, and God's creation.

DISCUSSION QUESTIONS

1. What is considered beautiful in this digital age?

2. How are images distorted digitally in the name of beauty?

3. How is the cross beautiful? How is the human body beautiful? How do society's definitions of beauty in this digital age contrast with beauty as described in the Bible?

4. What steps can you take to learn to see again, recognizing and focusing on true biblical beauty?

DO THIS, NOT THAT

LESS IS MORE

A hallmark of addiction is needing more and more of something in order to reach the same level of satisfaction. While one glass of wine used to do it for you, now it takes two or three glasses. Once upon a time, one pain pill was more than enough, but addiction requires multiple pain pills just to be content.

It is not a stretch to say that we are visually addicted. Radiant screens, billions of pixels, and endless color has caused us to be visual addicts. And as with any addiction, we need more and more of it to keep us satisfied. When it comes time to buy a new television, do you get a bigger one or a smaller one? When it comes time to get a new tablet, do you opt for the one with more or fewer pixels?

While we are all familiar with the adage "less is more," we often live as if "more is more." Consider these ways to foster a less-is-more approach:

- Adjust the settings on your smartphone or computer to gray scale. Spoiler alert: it will be the worst thing ever. However, doing this even for a short period of time will reveal your addiction to color on digital screens. With your devices set to gray scale, you will find that you use them far less.

- Do an inventory of the digital images that you produce every day. How and how often do you alter images before posting them? What do the changes that you make to these images say about how you feel about yourself? Why are you dissatisfied with yourself, loving yourself conditionally, when God loves you unconditionally?

- Go outside or to an art museum. These are places where you can develop your ability to see again. When outside or in a forest, you will see real color and sights rather than electronically produced color and sights. When at an art museum, you will see artwork that helps you see the world in new ways. Both of these experiences can be difficult at first, but over time they can be powerful antidotes to visual noise.

It may sound strange to say that we are visually addicted. Perhaps you disagree. Yet our ever enlarging televisions and multiplying megapixels would say otherwise. Although the consumer mentality of this world says more is more, you do not have to live that way. You can find beauty, simplicity, and peace in a life that sees more in less.

CHAPTER 9

MEMES, IMITATION, AND BEHAVIORAL CONTAGION

They called it the forbidden fruit.

But it was not a fruit—it was a laundry detergent pod. These pods are filled with soap, inedible and poisonous. Nevertheless, for a brief time in early 2018, intentionally consuming laundry detergent pods was a thing.

In only the first two weeks of 2018, thirty-nine teenagers intentionally ate laundry detergent pods. By way of comparison, there were thirty-nine incidents of this in all of 2016. In a brief two-week stretch, teenagers intentionally consumed the same amount of laundry detergent pods as are usually consumed in a fifty-two week stretch. Why the precipitous rise in teenagers salivating for soap?

Internet memes.

Long before intentionally ingesting laundry detergent pods was an internet challenge, there had been problems with people mistakenly consuming these pods. Very young children would find the liquid-filled pods and mistake them for candy. In 2015, the satirical newspaper *The Onion* published a fictitious op-ed piece online from the perspective of a young child extolling the tasty virtues of detergent pods. A few years later, in 2017, the notion of eating these laundry pods became a widely circulating internet joke. The notion of these pods as "forbidden fruit" came up on chat boards, social media posts, and videos. Then, in January 2018, consuming detergent pods became an internet challenge. This is when it became a crisis.

Internet challenges are simply dares issued and attempted through social media. In a typical internet challenge, someone will post a video on social media presenting a challenge of some sort; others see the video, attempt to do it themselves, and then post the results of their attempt, either failed or successful. The challenge often goes viral when others see the video of the challenge and imitate the same behavior. The Ice Bucket Challenge promoted awareness of amyotrophic lateral sclerosis (ALS) through videos in which people poured buckets of ice water over their heads. An example of a less noble and more hazardous internet challenge is the cinnamon challenge, in which someone must swallow a spoonful of cinnamon in under a minute without any water. As you would expect, this cinnamon challenge often ends in choking, vomiting, or puffing out clouds of brown dust like a cinnamon-breathing dragon.

Internet challenges are connected to a much broader phenomenon known as internet memes. Deriving its name from the Greek word *mimeme* ("imitated thing"), memes are imitations—whether it's an idea, a behavior, a joke, or a photo—that rapidly spread from person to person with slight modifications. For instance, a funny photo may circulate for a period of time on the internet. Eventually, someone will add some text to the photo and recast its original meaning. This will then be shared and modified by users across various platforms.

Memes are far more than just playful internet inventions. The imitation that drives internet memes—be it eating laundry detergent pods, rapidly ingesting a spoonful of cinnamon, or reposting adaptations of funny photos—reveals much about the human tendency to imitate the wants, thoughts, fears, and actions of others. Memes are more than just funny internet diversions; they are a window into the human heart and mind, soul and psyche.

NEGATIVE MIMESIS: EYES ON ONE ANOTHER

John Barclay, a New Testament scholar at the University of Durham, gave a lecture at Concordia Seminary in St. Louis that described how the age of the internet has altered the way people relate to one another and to God:

> In an age when people fear the judgment of their peers far more than they fear the judgment of God, we have become increasingly petulant, critical, even cruel, and it's proving hard to take. . . . Our contemporaries are not now primarily trying to win the favor of God; they are trying to win the favor of one another. The judgment they fear is not the last judgment, but humiliating comments on social media.[46]

According to Barclay, the digital technology that is so common in our modern world has had an impact on how many people think about God. That is to say, the horizon of humanity's gaze has shifted away from God and toward one another. And digital technology has done much to facilitate this shift.

The internet makes it easier than ever before to see what

---

46 John Barclay, "Paul, Grace, and Liberation from Human Judgments of Worth" (lecture, Concordia Seminary, St. Louis, MO, April 4, 2017), 6:03, 9:53, used by permission, https:// scholar.csl.edu/sem/Paul_Grace_and_Liberation_from_Human_Judgements_of_Worth /Paul_Grace_and_Liberation_from_Human_Judgements_of_Worth/1/.

others are doing or accomplishing. This leads us to envy and desire what others have and to imitate the thoughts and behaviors of people around us. Digital media are a veritable meme factory, pumping out a steady flow of envy, desire, and imitation.

The topics of envy, desire, and imitation quickly lead to the scholarly work of René Girard. Girard, a literary critic who later became an anthropologist and religious studies scholar, is well known for developing the concept of mimetic desire. According to this theory, human desire is based on imitating the desires of others. Desire is seldom a straight line in which a subject desires an object. Instead, we often rely on others to mediate our desires, creating a triangular relationship between subject, object, and mediators.[47]

We look to others—models of behavior—to determine what is desirable. For example, the laundry detergent pods we discussed earlier are not desirable in and of themselves; rather, they became desirable because other people apparently desired them enough to record themselves eating them. We desire what our model desires instead of desiring an object for its own sake.

Envy, therefore, figures heavily in Girard's theory of mimetic desire. Envy often leads to rivalry, and rivalry often leads to violence. These manifestations—envy, rivalry, violence—are usually categorized as examples of "bad mimesis" or "negative mimesis." In other words, these are examples of human beings not only imitating the desires of others but also clashing with one another over these mutually desired objects. A very simple illustration of this bad mimesis is a group of toddlers fighting over the same toy. The children want the toy largely because the others want the toy. Because others stand in the way of getting the desired toy, rivalry and fighting follow.

---

47 See René Girard, *Deceit, Desire, and the Novel* (Baltimore: Johns Hopkins Press, 1965).

Many scholars have used Girard's bad mimesis to help explain and understand human violence. Some theologians have connected negative mimesis to the fall of humanity and original sin. The serpent said to Eve, "Did God actually say, 'You shall not eat of any tree in the garden'?" (Genesis 3:1). In saying this, Satan presented God as a rival to His human creatures—God has something that you do not possess, and you should want this thing simply because God has it and you don't. Satan antagonistically invited human creatures to imitate God. The tragedy of Genesis 3 is that humanity began to see God as a rival, and bad mimesis ensued.

It should come as no surprise that following Adam and Eve's fall into sin, the rest of humanity falls into envy, desire, and violence. Genesis 4 tells how Cain envied God's acceptance of Abel's offering to the point that Cain was willing to act violently against his brother. Cain saw the relationship that his brother had with God and he wanted it. His envy and desire quickly transformed into rivalry and violence.

POSITIVE MIMESIS: EYES ON GOD

But mimesis does not have to be bad. Drawing on the concepts of Girard, several scholars and theologians have explored the possibility of positive mimesis. For example, Vittorio Gallese, a neuroscience professor, sees negative mimesis as only one side of the coin. Humans do have a capacity for empathy, love, and altruism. These traits can also be imitated so that Girard's theory of mimesis could be cast in a positive light, not just in the negative.[48]

---

48 Vittorio Gallese, "The Two Sides of Mimesis: Girard's Mimetic Theory, Embodied Simulation and Social Identification," *Journal of Consciousness Studies* 16, no. 4 (January 2009): 21–44, https://www.ingentaconnect.com/contentone/imp/jcs/2009/00000016/00000004 /art00002.

In other words, mimesis does not have to be bad and result in envy, rivalry, and violence. It is possible to use Girard's theory of mimetic desire to understand positive mimesis. Mimetic theory helps us understand the rampant envy, desire, and imitation that occurs on the internet; yet mimetic theory can also offer a path out of the envy, desire, and imitation that occurs in these digital spaces. The deep desire to imitate others can be directed toward desiring to imitate the triune God—Father, Son, and Holy Spirit.

Theologians such as Hans Urs von Balthasar, Bernard Lonergan, and Raymund Schwager have put Girard's mimetic theory into conversation with trinitarian theology. The three persons of the Trinity—Father, Son, and Holy Spirit—are eternally in perfect relationship or communion with one another. This relationship is known as *perichoresis*. No envious or bad mimesis exists among the persons of the Trinity. Rather, the persons of the Trinity exist in positive mimesis, living in loving union and joyous imitation of one another. Jesus pointed to this constant interaction and imitation between the persons of the Trinity:

> When the Spirit of truth comes, He will guide you into all the truth, for He will not speak on His own authority, but whatever He hears He will speak, and He will declare to you the things that are to come. He will glorify Me, for He will take what is Mine and declare it to you. All that the Father has is Mine; therefore I said that He will take what is Mine and declare it to you. (John 16:13–15)

The Trinity, specifically the perichoretic interaction of the Father, Son, and Holy Spirit, serves as the supreme representation of positive mimesis. Simply put, the Father, Son, and Holy Spirit reveal what it looks like to be in relationship without rivalry, envy, and antagonistic interaction. The triune God shows us what it looks like to imitate others in a positive, holy, and sinless way.

The doctrine of the Trinity reveals who God really is and, in a way, helps clarify who humans are. If God's human creatures have been made in the image of God (Genesis 1:27), then the doctrine of the Trinity informs and intersects with humanity on the basis of the image of God. God made us to be a reflection of Himself. Sin destroyed our human capacity to reflect God. In Christ Jesus, through the power of the Holy Spirit, our inability to imitate the Trinity has been transformed by the grace of God. Through the Means of Grace—the proclamation of the Gospel, the waters of Baptism, and the body and blood of Christ in the Lord's Supper—the Holy Spirit regenerates the image of God within us and enables us to be imitators of Him.

Being a new creation in Christ, receiving salvation from sin and the gracious recovery of the image of God, invites us into a life of positive mimesis: "Beloved, do not imitate evil but imitate good. Whoever does good is from God; whoever does evil has not seen God" (3 John 11). The Holy Spirit enables us to hear and heed the words of Jesus when He says, "Just as I have loved you, you also are to love one another" (John 13:34). Similarly, Paul frequently depicts the Christian life as being a life of positive mimesis: "Be imitators of me, as I am of Christ" (1 Corinthians 11:1). Paul counseled the Church in Thessalonica, saying:

> Now we command you, brothers, in the name of our Lord Jesus Christ, that you keep away from any brother who is walking in idleness and not in accord with the tradition that you received from us.

For you yourselves know how you ought to imitate
us, because we were not idle when we were with
you. (2 Thessalonians 3:6–7)

Finally, the Book of Hebrews offers a similar encouragement to imitate the lives of faithful people: "Remember your
leaders, those who spoke to you the word of God. Consider the
outcome of their way of life, and imitate their faith" (13:7). As
bearers of God's image, restored human creatures rightly imitate God when they desire what is good and live in a way that
imitates God's goodness. The imitation of God is never about
replacing God or even perfectly replicating God; rather, this
joyous imitation is about fully participating in the divine life
so that the people of God increasingly live in a way that reflects
God's will.

The bottom line is this: Negative mimesis sets our eyes on
others and imitates their sinful desires and behaviors. Positive mimesis sets our eyes on God and imitates His desires
and behaviors.

DIGITAL MIMESIS:
NEGATIVE, POSITIVE, OR BOTH?

Individuality has been a central concept in modern thought.
For the past couple hundred years, it has been popular to speak
of the autonomous individual who is entirely free to think, act,
and live according to his or her own desires. More recently,
however, some scholars have been influenced by the philosophy
of Ludwig Wittgenstein as well as postmodernism so as to question whether it's possible for an individual to be purely autonomous. Instead of thinking about people as individuals who are
free from the influence of others, it may be more constructive

to think of humans as being "interdividual." That is to say, every person is an individual constantly interacting with other individuals. You may be your own person, but the influence of other persons is entirely unavoidable.

This is overwhelmingly true when it comes to the internet. (Notice the similarities in the language of *internet* and *interdividual*.) Digital technologies facilitate hyperconnected interactions between people, including their opinions and behaviors. Consider the Netflix Effect, for example.

With the advent of streaming services such as Netflix, popular releases are often binge-watched by millions of people at the same time. *The Queen's Gambit* is a novel about a female chess player that was originally published in 1983. Nearly forty years after its original publication, Netflix created a miniseries based on the novel. As soon as the streaming service offered the series, several related digital phenomena occurred: Google searches on chess began trending, eBay and Amazon saw a precipitous spike in sales of chess sets, and online chess games and training exploded in popularity.

Chess has been around for nearly 1,500 years. But suddenly, everyone found out about this new thing called chess because of a show on Netflix. This is the Netflix Effect—an example of individuals living as interdividuals, people profoundly connected to and influenced by one another.

Is this a bad thing? Is there something wrong with seeing a show and becoming interested in chess? Long before Netflix, Bob Ross was on public television inspiring people to paint happy little squirrels and mountains. Was there anything wrong with that?

No. There is nothing inherently wrong with seeing what others are doing, finding it inspiring or interesting, and following in their patterns. Imitating others can be innocent or even good. As previously described, imitation does not always have to be negative or sinful. Imitation can be the basis for education and knowledge, creativity and culture.

However, imitation can clearly be harmful as well. Consider the concept of behavioral contagion from previous chapters. While imitation is sometimes a conscious choice, such as buying the same sneakers as others in a social group in order to gain acceptance, behavioral contagion is typically an unconscious process in which humans imitate a behavior after exposure to others performing it. Behavioral contagion can be as innocent as picking up the mannerisms and gestures of a peer group or as deadly as influencing one to commit suicide (a well-established phenomenon).

Behavioral contagion and imitation can also be harmful in subtle ways. While we may not immediately realize it, digital spaces especially invite us to imitate others in less than holy ways.

Are You Imitating Wants?

The internet has revolutionized marketing. Unlike traditional forms of marketing and advertising, digital marketing and internet advertising allow for extremely targeted campaigns. Billboards and magazine advertisements were rather imprecise tools for marketing products to consumers; a company had to hope that people driving by or reading a periodical cared about the products they were hoping to sell through an advertisement. However, the internet changed this by directing specific advertisements to users based on their search history, browser cookies, and likes on social media. The internet allows advertisers to market their products to consumers with laserlike focus. The 2002 movie *Minority Report* envisioned this type of advertising occurring in the "distant future" of 2054. This type of advertising is already commonplace today.

Marketing often relies on the concepts of mimetic desire to sell products. Companies make you want a product because someone else wants that product. Toothpaste is marketed to consumers by showing attractive, sexually desirable people using it. It is not the toothpaste that you want; instead, you want to be like the person who uses that toothpaste. Advertisers use the same principles to sell cars, shoes, and electronics. Constantly being bombarded with models for what we ought to want and desire can subtly create covetousness within us. And Jesus had something to say about coveting: "Take care, and be on your guard against all covetousness, for one's life does not consist in the abundance of his possessions" (Luke 12:15).

Are You Imitating Groups?

We seek out others on the internet who seem like us, who share common traits, or whom we would like to be. Many social media platforms have the option of forming and joining public or private groups. When we identify with others or a group, it implies that enough of a perceived kinship exists for the individual to embrace attributes of others. By embracing the attributes of the group, the individual person is transformed in the process. The need for affiliation, a phrase made popular by psychologist David McClelland, motivates this process. This need is characterized by the desire for a sense of involvement and belonging within a social group.

The stronger the desire for affiliation and the more regular the contact, the greater the potential to be influenced by others. This power can be abused to take advantage of individuals based on the illusion of having a relationship bond, when in reality someone may be simply exploiting others with ulterior motives. The individual seeking the approval of the group is rewarded for imitating the behaviors and way of thinking of the group. Yet the threat of loss of approval of the group with exclusion or shaming is also present. What is initially motivated by this affiliation goal eventually becomes automatic when the behaviors and thought processes are repeated over time.

Imitating the behaviors of a group can make it difficult to maintain self-awareness. People often gauge their behavior against the behaviors of others. Group dynamics can distort your perspective on what is truly normal or right. Things that are abnormal or unhealthy—for example, extreme violence in video games or verbally harassing others online—can be normalized within the dynamics of a group. We can get the false impression that "everyone is doing it" and that the majority of people approve of this way of being. This social pressure can also push us to act impulsively, behaving without first thinking about the ramifications of our actions.

Are You Imitating Lust?

The internet has also revolutionized lust. Pornography has made ample use of digital technology. Digital spaces have become overrun with obscene, offensive, and downright abusive depictions of sex. These images are not only on pornographic websites but also on the shows offered by various streaming services. Beyond pornographic content, digital spaces are also virtual playgrounds for lust. Social media platforms make it dangerously easy for married people to search out past boyfriends or girlfriends and to engage in private conversations that should not be happening. Dating apps invite users to swipe left or right based on little more than visual lust.

The pornography and lust found in digital spaces is closely related to mimetic desire. But this relationship between lust and imitation is nothing new. Canto 5 of Dante's *Inferno*, written in the 1300s, tells of the character Francesca in the circle of lust:

> One day we reading were for our delight
> Of Launcelot, how Love did him enthral.
> Alone we were and without any fear.
>
> Full many a time our eyes together drew
> That reading, and drove the colour from our faces;
> But one point only was it that o'ercame us.
>
> When as we read of the much-longed-for smile
> Being by such a noble lover kissed,
> This one, who ne'er from me shall be divided,
>
> Kissed me upon the mouth all palpitating.
> Galeotto was the book and he who wrote it.
> That day no farther did we read therein.[49]

Reading a book about an amorous encounter led Francesca and her lover, Paolo, to set the book down and imitate what they were reading. Similarly, the sinful lust that abounds on digital spaces easily translates into sinful thoughts and actions. Again, Jesus has something to say on this: "Everyone who looks at a woman with lustful intent has already committed adultery with her in his heart" (Matthew 5:28).

Are You Imitating Scorn?

Internet memes can be funny—really funny. However, behind those memes are real people. Many of the people who have

---

49 Dante Alighieri, *The Divine Comedy*, Inferno, canto 5, trans. Henry Wadsworth Longfellow, Project Gutenberg, August 1997, https://www.gutenberg.org/files/1001/1001-h/1001-h .htm#CantoV.

become internet memes did not willingly offer up their photos for that purpose. Embarrassing school photos leaked onto the internet, stock photos that later became viral jokes, and random photos taken of a person without his or her permission have all become internet memes.

More than just personal cost affects those whose faces are connected to the memes. Many internet memes are predicated on subtle forms of aggressive or negative humor. Someone's ridiculous photo makes you laugh because that person is a fool. A funny video often hinges on a person's overreaction or stupidity. Much of our laughter relies on having scorn for someone else. As with the previous topics, Jesus has something to say on this too: "Whoever insults his brother will be liable to the council; and whoever says, 'You fool!' will be liable to the hell of fire" (Matthew 5:22).

Are You Imitating Love, Grace, and Kindness?

Nevertheless, digital spaces can certainly provide us with opportunity to imitate godly love, grace, and kindness. The internet and social media can put us into contact with godly people worthy of our imitation. Some people—in fact, many people—exude God's love, grace, and kindness online. These individuals use digital spaces for the increase of Christ and the encouragement of others. These people post God's Word as well as words of wisdom. These people add beauty and grace to digital spaces.

Follow these people on social media. Like their posts. Imitate them as they imitate Christ: "Join in imitating me, and keep your eyes on those who walk according to the example you have in us" (Philippians 3:17).

CONCLUSION

Mimesis in its various forms permeates digital technology—from memes to challenges to contagion. While we cannot completely avoid the influence of others, especially in digital spaces, we can limit our exposure to negative influences and foster exposure to positive ones. Mimesis can be negative when we are led into envy, rivalry, and violence because of who we follow. Negative influence provokes the imitation of wants, lust, and scorn. Mimesis can be positive when it involves following God and godly people. Positive influence provokes the imitation of godly love, grace, and kindness.

DISCUSSION QUESTIONS

1. Think of some of your favorite internet memes, or do an internet search for popular memes. What is appealing about these memes? What motivates your appreciation of these memes? Is it envy, wants, or lust? Or is it love, grace, and kindness?

2. Identify one example of how digital technology influences the thoughts or behaviors of others.

3. Identify one source of negative mimesis for yourself and develop a plan for limiting that exposure or influence.

4. Think of ways to access digital technology resources for the purpose of positive mimesis, especially exposure to God. How could you be influenced in positive ways? How could you influence others in positive ways through expressions of love, grace, and kindness?

DO THIS, NOT THAT

FOLLOWING, FRIENDING, AND FEIGNING OTHERS

It is easy to assume that whom we follow or friend on social media platforms is of no significance. We may think that the websites we visit, the books we read, or the shows we watch have little sway over us. It does not matter who I frequently interact with via text or Snapchat.

The apostle Paul would disagree. He counseled Christians in Corinth, saying, "Do not be deceived: 'Bad company ruins good morals'" (1 Corinthians 15:33). It appears that Paul was actually quoting the Greek playwright Menander with these words.[50] As he often did, Paul found a true saying or sentiment within his contemporary culture and showed how it aligned with God's truth. Both common wisdom and the Word of God agree: be aware of whom you follow or friend. Whether you realize it or not, you are likely to feign the behaviors of these individuals.

The people that we follow and friend, read and watch, celebrate and communicate with have an influence over us. As such, we should be deliberate and thoughtful about whom we allow to influence us.

Cull negative influences. Bookshelves, web browser book-marks, friends and people you follow are like toenails—they should be trimmed every now and then. In the moment, it seemed like a good idea to follow that hateful political pundit. When you first saw the request, it seemed fine to accept that

---

50 See Gregory J. Lockwood, *1 Corinthians*, Concordia Commentary (St. Louis: Concordia Publishing House, 2000), 579.

friend request from your high school boyfriend or girlfriend from a long time ago. Bookmarking that celebrity gossip website appeared to be a good move when you first did it. Yet on further consideration, all of these turned out to be horrible ideas. At least once a year, you should cull the negative influences in your life. (*Cull*, not *call*; that would be the opposite of what we are suggesting.) Drop some "friends" (who are really not your friends) from Facebook. Unfollow some folks on Twitter. Get rid of some books that probably should not be sitting on your bookshelf, and block a few websites while you are at it.

Beware of influencers. The internet has created a crazy new occupation known as "influencer." Sometimes internet influencers are supermodels paid to post about a new line of makeup. Sometimes internet influencers can take the shape of a ten-year-old child with a maniacal grin unwrapping a new toy on a YouTube video while other children longingly watch and want the same toy. (It's a strange place out there.) No matter what form, beware of any individual on the internet who seeks to influence you in ways that are not godly. Be wary of individuals with high numbers of followers and who receive monetary gain for promoting products. To quote Aristotle, "A friend to all is a friend to none."

Drop everyone? Didn't Jesus hang out with people who might be bad influences? He spent time with salty fishermen, tax collectors, and zealots. Should Christians create a hermetically sealed environment in digital spaces? No. Cloistering ourselves off from people who do not know Jesus makes it rather difficult to tell people about Jesus. Rather, followers of Jesus should be deliberate and conscientious of those with whom they are interacting in digital spaces and why. You may choose to follow someone on social media even if that person lives in a way that is contrary to God's will. You might determine that interacting with a friend or family member opposed to the Christian faith is prudent. That's all right. The key is to give some thought to these interactions and individuals. Rather than mindlessly following and friending people, know what you are doing and why. Be aware that although you might be influencing this person, influence is often a two-way interchange. He or she may also be influencing you.

Influence is inevitable. Although we like to think of ourselves as individuals, we are interconnected individuals constantly influencing one another. This can take a positive or negative shape. The difference, though, is in being aware of the who and the how of this influence: Who is influencing you? How are you being influenced?

CHAPTER 10

CLOWNS AND PRINCES, USERS AND DEVELOPERS

Theater was to Elizabethan England what Netflix is to modern life. The British of the Early Modern Age binge-watched Shakespeare with the same fervor that we binge-watch British cooking shows. In sixteenth-century London, the theater was a popular form of amusement that transcended wealth, education, and social standing.

In a time before internet or smartphones, the theater attracted a wide range of people and social classes. Yet theater-goers were separated by class within the theater itself. The "cheap seats" did not even come with seats. Known as *groundlings*, the lowest-paying patrons stood in an open-air pit in the middle of the theater. The pit, also known as the yard, was without seats and without a roof or covering, and so it was subject to scorching sunshine or pouring rain. (But then again, it only cost a penny to attend the theater as a groundling.) The more expensive seats were those in the gallery; these included a roof, a seat, and sometimes even a cushion. Finally, the most expensive seats—those reserved for the nobility, aristocracy, and powerful individuals—included private galleries and were practically on the stage itself.

The nobles, the groundlings, and everyone in between

gathered together to watch a play at the theater. With such diverse throngs of people in attendance, there was a strong sense that the theater was a distillation of life and society as a whole. Shakespeare's Globe Theatre derived its name to some degree from the notion of *theatrum mundi* (literally, "the world stage"). The idea of the world stage supposed that the stage was a summation of life in this world. In fact, the architecture of the physical space was a microcosm of the globe: the area above the stage was referred to as the heavens, the space underneath the stage was known as hell, and the stage was where life was acted out between the clutches of heaven and hell for all the world to see.

PRINCES AND CLOWNS, TECHNOLOGISTS AND USERS

Shakespeare did far more than entertain people with his plays. He also played with the social structure of his day. In *Hamlet*, the very same play in which Shakespeare coined the phrase *groundlings*, he challenged societal expectations by making a prince look like a dimwit while a clown came off looking like a genius.

Prince Hamlet is by far the wittiest of all Shakespeare's characters. This young prince has a sharp tongue and a precocious intellect. Throughout the entire play, Hamlet is constantly flipping the script on others, making a play of their words, and just being an all-around cheeky guy. And yet Prince Hamlet meets his match in scene 1 of act 5 when he happens upon a common gravedigger.

Hamlet enters a graveyard and finds a gravedigger singing while preparing a grave. Shocked by the gravedigger's cheerful demeanor, Hamlet says, "Has this fellow no feeling of his business, that he sings at grave-making?"[51] This gravedigger—also called a clown, which was a common name for comic relief characters—is digging dirt, tossing up skulls, and singing songs. Hamlet strikes up a conversation with this gravedigging clown.

Thinking that this common man is obtuse and unaware, Hamlet asks whose grave it is at which the gravedigger toils. With this simple question, a duel of witticisms begins. With every question that Hamlet asks, the gravedigger is a few steps ahead of the prince. Although he is standing knee-deep in a grave and covered in dirt and sweat, this common clown of a man reveals that he is of faster thought, clearer perception, and sharper tongue than Prince Hamlet.

All of this leads Hamlet finally to declare in exasperation, "The toe of the peasant comes so near the heel of the courtier that he galls his kibe."[52] To translate for those of us who do not often talk about galling (irritating) and kibe (inflammation of the heel), Hamlet is saying that common gravediggers are just as perceptive and smart as aristocrats.

What does this conversation between a gravedigger and a prince have to do with technology? Just as this common clown was wittier than an educated prince, users of technology are often a few steps ahead of technologists. The people signing the user agreements are not necessarily less perceptive than those who create the technology.

Silicon Valley contains many technological princes and princesses. These technologists are responsible for inventing many of the technologies that we use on a daily basis: personal computers, video games, social media, apps, and much more. These technological marvels may leave us with the impression

---

51 William Shakespeare, *Hamlet*, act 5, scene 1, Project Gutenberg, November 1998, https://www.gutenberg.org/files/1524/1524-h/1524-h.htm#sceneV_1.

52 Shakespeare, *Hamlet*.

that the royalty of Silicon Valley know significantly more than common clowns such as us. We are tempted to think that they are more perceptive, faster thinking, and generally a few steps ahead of us.

However, this would be a crucial error. Whether we are high or low, wealthy or not, God invites all of us to locate our hope in the certainty of His promises: "As for the rich in this present age, charge them not to be haughty, nor to set their hopes on the uncertainty of riches, but on God, who richly provides us with everything to enjoy" (1 Timothy 6:17). We so easily forget that creators of technology, like all of us, are fully fallible and deeply dependent upon God for all good things.

As users of technology, sort of like the groundlings in the theater, we are subjected to the decisions of Silicon Valley inventors. Cloistered together in their own private gallery, these powerful technologists create products that they hope users will want, purchase, and use. Despite the apparent chasm separating users and technologists, groundlings and nobility, these princes and princesses are not always as perceptive and smart as we might think.

For example, Apple released its comprehensive health app in 2014. According to Craig Federighi, an Apple software executive, the health app monitored all the metrics that users were most interested in: blood pressure, activity levels, sleep patterns, and body weight. It even allowed users to track more obscure metrics such as blood alcohol content, sodium intake, and inhaler use for people with asthma. It did absolutely everything under the sun—except allow female users to track their menstrual cycles. Logically, half of users would be interested in this function. Women have been monitoring their menstrual cycles since time immemorial. Omitting this feature on a health app revealed the fallibility of the (mostly male) Silicon Valley technologists and frankly made them look pretty obtuse. As a result of widespread user dissatisfaction, a menstrual cycle tracking feature has since been added to the app.

On the other side of the equation, users have contributed much to Silicon Valley technologies. For example, many important aspects of Twitter's user interface came from actual users. Features such as the @ and # symbols on Twitter came from people using the service. The retweet and thread functions were also ideas generated by users, not highly paid Twitter developers. In this sense, ordinary users play an important part in developing the technologies that they use.

Omitting obvious features from their technological creations is one thing. However, something even more alarming is occurring among the princes and princesses of Silicon Valley: many of them are opting out when it comes to using their own creations.

Mark Zuckerberg, Facebook's founder and CEO, encouraged his employees to "move fast and break things." Facebook and other Silicon Valley companies have proved that they are adept at quickly wreaking havoc in all areas of life. Their propensity to break things in a hurry has become clear over the past two decades.

Curiously, in the wake of all this disruptive technology, many Silicon Valley tech czars are concerned about the mess they are making. As briefly discussed in chapter 4, Sean Parker, Tim Cook, and Chamath Palihapitiya have all expressed concerns that Silicon Valley creations are indeed moving too fast and breaking far too many things. Others could also be added to this list:

- Twitter CEO Jack Dorsey has expressed grave

concerns about the heart-shaped like buttons that are ubiquitous on social media platforms. At the 2018 WIRED25 conference, Dorsey said, "Right now we have a big Like button with a heart on it and we're incentivizing people to want to drive that up. . . . Is that the right thing?"[53]

- Athena Chavarria, former executive assistant at Facebook, has expressed how she thinks that "the devil lives in our phone" and that phones can be destructive to children.[54]

- Jaron Lanier is widely considered one of the founders of virtual reality technology. He argues in his book *Dawn of the New Everything: Encounters with Reality and Virtual Reality* that virtual reality will test us as a society by amplifying human proclivities; he fears that the medium is extremely "vulnerable to creepiness."[55]

This list is not exhaustive, yet even this incomplete list makes it clear that the princes and princesses of Silicon Valley are prone to falling out of love with the inventions they so lovingly created. Meanwhile, many ordinary people—everyday consumers and users of these technologies—have had such reservations from the very beginning. Proverbs 14:12 is exactly on the mark: "There is a way that seems right to a man, but its end is the way to death."

---

53 Jack Dorsey, "Jack Dorsey on Filter Bubbles, Twitter Fights and 12 Years of Tweeting," interview by Nick Thompson, WIRED25 Conference, October 16, 2018), 16:33, https://www .wired.com/video/watch/wired25-twitter-ceo-jack-dorsey.

54 Nellie Bowles, "A Dark Consensus about Screens and Kids Begins to Emerge in Silicon Valley," *The New York Times*, October 26, 2018, https://www.nytimes.com/2018/10/26 /style/phones-children-silicon-valley.html.

55 Jaron Lanier, *Dawn of the New Everything* (New York: Henry Holt, 2017), 1.

MARTIN LUTHER'S
MESSAGE TO SILICON VALLEY

Whether you are a gravedigger or a prince, you have a vocation. God has called each of us to many different vocations. These callings from God are far more than mere occupations; rather, vocations are those tasks, responsibilities, offices, and relationships to which God calls each of us: "Only let each person lead the life that the Lord has assigned to him, and to which God has called him" (1 Corinthians 7:17).

While other Reformation theologians addressed the matter, Martin Luther has long been regarded as the leading theologian on the topic of vocation. Luther explained the doctrine of vocation to show that all legitimate forms of work—farming, soldiering, mothering, governing, and the list goes on—are callings from God. God calls each of us to different vocations, such as doctor, teacher, church member, citizen, neighbor, parent, spouse, pastor, child, and so forth. While vocations such as technologist, programmer, developer, technology manager, web designer, social media manager, and chief technology officer did not exist in the time of the Reformation, these are all examples of modern vocations.

Contrary to previous medieval formulations of vocation, which claimed that only religious work was a divine calling, Luther recognized that nonreligious forms of work are also divine callings that are pleasing to God and full of dignity. Luther developed a theology of work that understood that God looms behind human workers and their labor. Luther called human vocations a "mask of God," in which God is present and active through the work of ordinary people.[56] Since it was first

---

56 For more on this, see the classic text by Gustaf Wingren, *Luther on Vocation*, trans. Carl Rasmussen (Philadelphia: Muhlenberg Press, 1957).

articulated nearly five hundred years ago, Luther's theology of vocation has influenced generations of theologians.

Although it has long been the primary theological paradigm for understanding work, vocation has recently come under scrutiny by some theologians such as Jacques Ellul, John Howard Yoder, and more recently Miroslav Volf.[57] These theologians have argued that Luther's doctrine of vocation is unhelpful and perhaps even dangerous to modern society. Volf, in his book *Work in the Spirit*, argues that vocation does not address what human beings *should* desire their work to be and does not help make positive changes in work.

According to Volf, the doctrine of vocation is unable to overcome problems such as dehumanizing working conditions, nor can it keep powerful people accountable. According to this critique, if God has called you to be a cobalt miner in the Congo supplying material for iPhone batteries, then you can do nothing to rectify this matter; your job is to do your duty and be obedient to your boss. Conversely, if God has called you to be a powerful technology executive, then God wills you to this vocation and there is little that anyone—especially the cobalt miners or lowly individual users of technology—can say against you since you have been called to this vocation by God; your job is to wield your power, keep the stock price high, and subject others to your decisions.

Is this really the case? Is vocation unable to keep powerful leaders accountable? Does vocation really just encourage people to remain where they are in society and simply endure alienating and dehumanizing occupations while permitting powerful people to exercise their office without any accountability?

---

57 See Jacques Ellul, *The Ethics of Freedom* (Grand Rapids, MI: Eerdmans, 1976), and John Howard Yoder, *The Priestly Kingdom: Social Ethics as Gospel* (Notre Dame, IN: University of Notre Dame Press, 1984).

Contrary to these recent critiques, vocation can address the issues of these princes and princesses of Silicon Valley and the ordinary people using their creations.

Luther's treatise "The Freedom of a Christian," while not explicitly concerned with the topic of vocation, is an important text within this conversation. Luther makes two central arguments throughout the treatise: "A Christian is a perfectly free lord of all, subject to none. A Christian is a perfectly dutiful servant of all, subject to all."[58] Luther argues that Christians are free from working for their salvation yet bound to work for others. Faith in Christ Jesus makes one both free and bound, lord and servant, unbeholden and obligated.

While recognizing the complete freedom that we have in Christ, Luther simultaneously emphasizes the obligation of service to neighbors:

> A man does not live for himself alone in this mortal body to work for it alone, but he lives also for all men on earth; rather, he lives only for others and not for himself. To this end he brings his body into subjection that he may the more sincerely and freely serve others.[59]

But Luther's understanding of obligation and subjection is not limited to those in lowly positions with limited agency. Luther did not say that servants and laborers are called to a life of servitude while rulers and supervisors are called to a life of being served. Instead, God calls all to a life of service regardless of social status, power, or agency.

Our work is a vital act through which we can serve others. Whether you are a prince or a peasant, a Silicon Valley

---

58 LW 31:344.
59 LW 31:364.

technologist or the sad sap signing the user agreement, Luther implored all people "to serve, help, and in every way deal with his neighbor as he sees that God through Christ has dealt and still deals with him."[60] The implications of these words are radical for those in positions of power and authority. We expect servants and laborers to serve, help, and attend to the needs of others, but we do not expect rulers, supervisors, or business leaders to serve, help, and attend to the needs of others. Yet this is exactly what vocation is all about. God's calling for a life of neighborly servitude ascends to the highest places of power and authority within society.

On many occasions, Luther specifically addressed the vocational responsibilities of those in positions of power and authority. In his treatise "Temporal Authority," he called rulers and executors of power to serve with Christlike humility:

> [The ruler] should picture Christ to himself, and say, "Behold, Christ, the supreme ruler, came to serve me; He did not seek to gain power, estate, and honor from me, but considered only my need, and directed all things to the end that I should gain power, estate, and honor from Him and through Him. I will do likewise, seeking from my subjects not my own advantage but theirs. I will use my office to serve and protect them, listen to their problems and defend them, and govern to the sole end that they, not I, may benefit and profit from my rule."[61]

Luther often confronted people in power, and he was never shy about addressing their faults and shortcomings as leaders.

---

60 LW 31:366.
61 LW 45:120.

The concept of vocation makes it clear that powerful leaders must recognize the unique vocational responsibilities that accompany their leadership positions. Even if one is not a Christian, every person still possesses vocations and has been called by God to various places of service. It is not as if a Buddhist social media CEO does not have the vocation of CEO, spouse, parent, citizen, and neighbor. The difference is that Christians have an awareness that non-Christians do not have when it comes to God's work in and through them. Christians are aware of the divinely appointed responsibility that comes with a vocation. Both Christians and non-Christians, however, have God-given responsibilities that come with their vocations.

So it is not hard to imagine Luther calling on the likes of Jack Dorsey, Mark Zuckerberg, and Jeff Bezos to adopt a new personal dictum: "I will use my office to serve and protect others, listen to their problems and defend them, and govern to the sole end that they, not I, may benefit from my rule."

THE NARROWING GAP BETWEEN COMMONER AND ROYALTY

As mentioned at the beginning of this chapter, Shakespeare brilliantly depicted fictional commoners besting royalty on stage while real-life commoners and royalty watched. What he depicted on stage must have given some hope to the lowly groundlings in the pit. In this regard, modern technology is not unlike the interchange between Hamlet and the common gravedigger. The chasm between powerful technologists and ordinary people using technology is not as vast or insurmountable as we might suppose.

Postindustrial society, the shift that happened in the 1970s as Western society moved from a largely manufacturing-based economy to a largely service-based economy, has changed much of modern life. Among many other changes, this shift has changed the way people work, creating whole new industries and occupations. One upside is that the cost of entry for aspiring technologists is relatively low. Rather than needing to obtain a manufacturing plant, machines, and massive capital, entrepreneurs can pursue creative endeavors on a laptop or tablet. A relatively small amount of equipment—computers, hard drives, microphones, cameras, editing software—can allow someone to become an inventor or content creator. Some computer coding knowledge and plenty of determination can become an opportunity to change the world.

Twitter is an example of this development. Jack Dorsey was an undergraduate student at New York University working with a podcasting company. He had an idea for an SMS (short message service) communication platform. Once the basic coding was completed, Dorsey's first tweet was on March 21, 2006. He published a stunningly boring message: "just setting up my twttr." Soon thereafter, Dorsey made a habit of tweeting to his mother about what he was having for lunch. It all started as a rather insignificant project with relatively limited capital and equipment. Today, world leaders and organizations turn to Twitter to make some of their most important announcements.

Some scholars have described this shift as participatory culture. Henry Jenkins, a media scholar at the University of Southern California, has described participatory culture as having low barriers to content creation, opportunities to share one's creations with others, collaboration with other content creators, and meaningful discourse among various participants. Podcasting, video publishing, and open source software are just a few examples of participatory culture. In each of these examples, individuals can become active social agents with few barriers to participation. These platforms allow people to participate in creating and exchanging content and ideas in meaningful ways. The Good News of Jesus can be shared and communities can be bettered through these creative endeavors.

The notion of participatory culture is playing with some well-worn societal distinctions. For instance, the concept of user and consumer is becoming blurred. Users are generating content and becoming producers. Consumers are not just passively consuming products made by others but remixing and publishing their own creative contributions. These consumers may even become powerful themselves, such as YouTube stars and influencers, and they take on considerable responsibility for how they wield their power and influence. Some have even proposed the term *prosumer* rather than *consumer* to reflect how consumers now produce content as well as consume it. Some of this content just might change the world.

The point? A computer, some basic knowledge, lots of determination, and a great idea to love and serve neighbors can be a powerful combination for good in this world: "He has told you, O man, what is good; and what does the LORD require of you but to do justice, and to love kindness, and to walk humbly with your God?" (Micah 6:8).

CONCLUSION

Plays are places for play. In one sense, the theater is just playing around while people pretend and imagine. Yet in another sense, plays have a powerful ability to play around with our expectations and established ways of thinking. Shakespeare was a master at these sort of plays that played with expectations, disrupted the status quo, and broke with existing patterns in society.

In the same way, modern technology is playing with many of our expectations and established ways of thinking. Modern technology plays with the status quo: users end up having keener insight and better ideas than those who created the technology in the first place. Lowly commoners, the people signing the user agreements, are not the only ones who have a duty to serve others; the technologists who rule over Silicon Valley have an equal responsibility to serve and protect others, leading in such a way that others benefit from their work. And emerging technologies are actively playing with the divide between producer and consumer.

Jesus does much more than play with the established patterns of the world; He turned the world upside down with the cross and the empty tomb. In turn, the earliest followers of Jesus were accused of having "turned the world upside down" (Acts 17:6) as they lived out His teachings and proclaimed His message of salvation. The world accused Christ's followers of moving fast and breaking things as they proclaimed the Gospel. The disruptive message of the empty tomb and the forgiveness of sins has the power to change everything: power and status, guilt and regret, the past and the present, the future and eternity, life and death. By the power of the Holy Spirit, this message continues to transform you in Christ Jesus into one who is both free and bound, wanting for nothing while depending on Jesus for everything.

DISCUSSION QUESTIONS

1. What are some of your many different vocations? If you are discussing this question in a group, what vocations do you have in common and what vocations are unique to you?

2. In what ways do you serve others through your vocation? Whom do you serve in your vocations? How is God at work in and through this service?

3. How does the idea of vocation hold people in positions of power accountable?

4. Are there any ways that you produce media content and not just consume it? If so, how might you use this as a way to love and serve others through what you produce?

DO THIS, NOT THAT

LEARN SOMETHING NEW

Magic tricks appear to be magical. At first glance, we have no idea how they work: How did I have that quarter in my ear without knowing it? How does that rabbit stay so still inside that hat? And why does that poor lady keep on going into that box and letting them cut her in half on stage?

Once you learn how a magic trick works, it makes much more sense: The quarter was up the sleeve. The rabbit sits in a cage. The lady in the box is actually two ladies in two boxes. Learning the trick makes it much harder to be duped in the future.

While it's not possible to learn all the tricks of digital technology, you can learn a few. An incredible number of resources are available to expand your knowledge about digital technology. Consider doing one of the following:

Learn the basics of computer programming. Unless you are planning a future in computer programming or you are really interested in the topic, you do not need to become an expert in a programming language. However, it is well worth your time to learn something about the magic behind the technology we use on a daily basis. This is not unlike knowing the basics of car mechanics: most drivers know how to check or add oil to a car, change a flat tire, install a new headlight, and so forth. Why do many drivers know this? Well, if you're going to drive a car on a regular basis, it helps to know some basic things about how it works. The same goes for websites, apps, and computer programs. Accessible opportunities (such as Lynda.com or Khan Academy) abound to learn the basics of computer programming languages such as Python or Java. You don't have to become an expert, but at least learn some of the tricks behind all the magic.

Create something of your own. Making your own website, blog, or podcast is easy. Even if you consider yourself inept when it comes to technology, creating something online is not beyond your abilities. In all likelihood, only your mom will go to your website or listen to your podcast (yay, moms!)—that's all right. The point is not to attract tons of traffic or have millions of listeners. Rather, the experience of planning it out, putting it together, and sharing it with the world is very valuable. As with learning the basics of computer programming, creating is a way that you can learn some of the tricks of digital technology and be harder to dupe in the future.

Proverbs 18:15 tells us, "An intelligent heart acquires knowledge, and the ear of the wise seeks knowledge." Curiosity, lifelong learning, and growing in wisdom are good gifts of God, and they can be powerful forces for good in this world.

HANGING ON BY A CABLE

In the fourteenth century, Giovanni Boccaccio wrote *The Decameron* as the Black Death swept through Florence, Italy. In the eighteenth century, Daniel Defoe wrote *A Journal of the Plague Year* as the plague ravaged London. In the twentieth century, Albert Camus wrote *La Peste* ("The Plague") in the wake of several cholera epidemics in Algeria.

Like these other books, this one was written during a pandemic. (That is about all this book has in common with them, however; we are not suggesting that Boccaccio, Defoe, or Camus should move over and make room for us.) The development and initial writing of this book began before the COVID-19 pandemic took hold around the world in early 2020. The latter parts of this book were composed after the COVID-19 pandemic became a global event that altered life in both large and small ways.

Writing a book about technology during a pandemic can lead to some cognitive dissonance. While we are painfully aware of the problems presented by many modern technologies, we have also come to recognize the many virtues that they have to offer. For many people, digital technology became an umbilical cord connecting us to the outside world. Access to family and friends, work and education, groceries and health care were all mediated by digital technologies and the internet.

Were it not for these things, enduring a pandemic would have been far more difficult.

This epilogue briefly explores how technology can be helpful, especially in times of crisis or isolation. While the problems remain, the possibilities become very apparent.

DURABLE CABLES IN TIMES OF CRISIS

While there was not one single person or precipitating event behind the invention of the internet, a few key people and moments stand out. One of these individuals is an electrical engineer named Paul Baran. In 1959, against the backdrop of the long-standing threat of nuclear war, Baran proposed a durable communication network capable of surviving nuclear assault. The primary means of communication in that day—long-distance telephone systems—relied on centralized switching facilities. If one of these centralized facilities were destroyed, a whole swath of the system would fail. This made these telephone systems extremely vulnerable. So Baran designed a way to route information through a decentralized network of unmanned nodes. This idea played a key part in creating the internet.

In a way, the internet was made for times of crisis. While the nuclear threats of the Cold War era have waned, other crises remain. This global pandemic revealed the centrality of this decentralized network. It is no surprise that coronavirus quarantines resulted in a precipitous rise in internet usage. People began using internet technologies in new ways. While some people had previously used the internet for health care, education, or video conferencing with family, the COVID-19 pandemic made these uses much more common.

TELEMEDICINE

A mother, worried about her sick child, talks to the doctor on the telephone. She holds the baby up, and it coughs into the receiver. The doctor reassures her, and they all sleep peacefully that night. The year? 2020? No. The year was 1879.

A patient receives her regularly scheduled examination. The doctor reports that all vital signs are stable and gives a clean bill of health. The doctor? On Earth. The patient? In outer space.

The COVID-19 pandemic has seen an explosion in telemedicine, the use of technology for the remote assessment and treatment of patients. With the need for safe physical distancing so that doctors and patients do not contaminate one another, the number of telemedicine visits around the world has risen dramatically, especially in the United States. Telemedicine can connect a doctor with a patient in the next room, an urban doctor with a rural patient, a radiologist in Australia with a patient in New York City, and a doctor on Earth with an astronaut traveling in outer space.

The concept of telemedicine is not new. The case of the telephone being used to assess and treat a coughing baby appears in *The Lancet* from 1879.[62] However, the concept of telemedicine goes back even farther in time, as far back as ancient hieroglyphs and scrolls or farther. From those humble beginnings, telemedicine advanced through different forms, including sticks, smoke signals, letters, and telegrams, before arriving at the electronic communication of today, which includes videoconferencing, remote patient monitoring (RPM), and electronic medical records.

RPM involves the use of mobile medical devices and

---

62   Rashid L. Bashshur et al., "The Empirical Foundations of Telemedicine Interventions for Chronic Disease Management," *Telemedicine and e-Health* 20, no. 9 (September 2014): 769–800, https://doi.org/10.1089/tmj.2014.9981.

technology to obtain patient-generated health data, which is sent to health-care professionals for review. For example, a digital stethoscope converts acoustic sounds on the patient's end to electronic signals that are transmitted to the provider. Electronic medical records allow storage and retrieval of medical information for both providers and patients, refilling of medications, and direct messaging between providers and patients. Medical images, such as X-rays, scans, and electrocardiograms, can also be shared electronically.

The explosion of telemedicine in the United States during the COVID-19 pandemic was aided by a combination of reduced restrictions on its use and increased funding to support its practice. With less regulation and more reimbursement, telemedicine thrived. Even though telemedicine has existed for a while, it is now treated as equivalent to traditional in-person care, or at least as an acceptable substitute.

Studies have consistently demonstrated that clinical assessments, outcomes, and patient satisfaction are comparable between telemedicine and in-person care. Psychiatry is especially suited to the telemedicine format—in fact, after radiology, it's the most used form of telemedicine. Telepsychiatry, the delivery of psychiatric care through telecommunications technology, was a well-established practice prior to the coronavirus pandemic. With psychiatry's emphasis on talking to the patient and reduced reliance on physical examination, the necessary transition from traditional in-person care to telepsychiatry was easy.

Telemedicine has many advantages to traditional in-person care. Telemedicine safely bridges the physical distance between two parties. This is vitally important because there is a shortage of primary care physicians nationwide and an uneven distribution of the workforce, most pronounced in rural areas.

Telemedicine is cost-effective. Providers have fewer overhead expenses, and patients save money with fewer travel expenses and lost wages. Providers also note fewer missed appointments. What does a provider do when a patient doesn't show for the scheduled videoconference? After a few minutes alone online, the provider calls the patient, and in most instances the patient, having had technical issues or having forgotten about the appointment, joins the call.

Telemedicine is not without its areas of concern. With sensitive personal medical information, privacy concerns must be considered. For example, the majority of mobile health apps do not have privacy policies. And nobody wants to get "Zoombombed," especially when exposed mentally or physically. Telemedicine may also impact the patient-physician relationship negatively. Patients already complained prior to the pandemic that their physicians spent more time looking at computer screens than at the patients. Physicians complained that they spent more time with the electronic medical records than they did with their patients. Spending time with patients is the most rewarding part of a medical career, and more time with electronic medical records means less job satisfaction. During a pandemic, it seems like everything goes digital, and we are all staring at screens all the time. This only heightens the stress on the doctor-patient relationship.

Inadequate access to technology is also a significant barrier to quality care. Some Americans do not have access to the internet at all, and many lack the broadband, high-speed internet necessary for video calls and other important aspects of telemedicine. The most prominent discrepancies in access to the technology necessary for telemedicine are seen with age (older patients) and income (poverty). Because of the potential pitfalls, health technology should not be used for technology's sake. However, when used purposefully and equitably, health technology can be a powerful and even lifesaving tool.

ONLINE LEARNING

While telemedicine safely brings together patients and health-care professionals, online learning safely brings together teachers and students of all ages. At times during the pandemic, everyone from kindergartners on up to medical, seminary, and law students have attended classes online. While online learning is far from perfect, what's a safer option during a pandemic? Can't live with online learning? Or can't live without it?

Good online learning overcomes the barrier of physical distance by reducing transactional distance. The theory of transactional distance, developed by Dr. Michael G. Moore in the 1970s, recognizes nonphysical forms of distance, such as social, psychological, and relational distance. Transactional distance is reduced through meaningful online interactions. Students are no longer passive recipients of information, vessels to be filled with the knowledge of teachers. A world of information is already at the fingertips of these students. Students are now independent explorers in need of learning experiences, which may include peer-to-peer or faculty-led small groups (often accomplished through videoconferencing breakout rooms), multimedia content, audience response systems, quizzes, and private chat questions, especially advantageous for socially anxious students. During live, in-person lectures, perhaps a couple of hands go up, and maybe a couple of students approach the professor after class. During online lectures, a stream of chat questions, some anonymous, come in throughout the lesson.

This time of online learning demands flexibility. Teachers

have the challenge of instructing students "Zoombified" by up to eight hours of staring at the flickering lights of screens. These students are stressed by school closures, canceled social events, and lower study efficiency and motivation with online learning. These types of stresses necessitate a little more grace and a lot more flexibility with what is expected of teachers and students. This includes more flexible rules in the home for total screen time. Just because children are on screens most of the day for school does not mean they should be banned from all additional screen use. The previous pediatric recommendation of two hours or less a day of screen time just does not cut it during a pandemic. Being online for learning has a different function than being online for video games or video chats with friends.

Ideally, when no longer in a time of pandemic, the best aspects of both telemedicine and online learning are preserved. Hybrid models include the right mix of the in-person and virtual aspects of medicine and instruction. Without the pressure of a pandemic, use of technology can be dictated by best practice, not by necessity. But with the limiting pressure of a pandemic, much of our living is online.

SOCIAL SUPPORT

In addition to medicine and education, digital tools can also positively impact mental health by providing social support. Social support plays a key role in mental wellness, but it's often in short supply while we are social distancing, making it even harder to cope with a crisis. Fortunately, digital technology can promote wellness by allowing us to keep in touch with friends and family and better cope with adversity. Isolation worsens mental wellness through the pain of loneliness.

Children and adolescents, as well as the elderly, are at

increased risk of depression and anxiety from the social isolation encountered during quarantine. For children and adolescents, the greater the divide between their age-appropriate elevated desire for social contact and their actual social contact, the greater the loneliness. Quarantine comes at a particularly inopportune time for youth, whose phase of development requires peers for identity and support.

While videoconferencing is often the best that we can do during a pandemic to allow face-to-face contact, it is not the same as being together in person. The time delays, constant interruptions when two people try to talk at the same time, indirect eye contact, distraction of seeing ourselves during the interaction, weird lighting, lost calls, and partial bodies with limited nonverbal cues all remind us that we are not truly sharing the same space.

Digital communications also lack touch. Behavioral scientist Harry Harlow demonstrated the importance of touch in human life with his now-famous surrogate mother experiment. Harlow showed that infant monkeys who received ample touch thrived, while those deprived of touch experienced diminished health and well-being. The infant monkeys that were touched by their mothers did the best. Meanwhile, other infant monkeys had objects to hold as surrogate mothers, some made of soft foam and cloth and others composed of wires. The monkeys that had access to soft objects fared better than the ones with wire objects. Harlow made a compelling case for the importance of touch and close contact with another.

We crave human touch with pressure and skin-to-skin contact. It provides feelings of safety, trust, and calm. Human touch activates the vagus nerve, which slows our heart rate and lowers our blood pressure. It also causes release of oxytocin, the "love hormone." More specifically, oxytocin helps us feel emotionally close to and bonded with others.

Despite its lack of touch and physical contact, videoconferencing has been used in ways unique to the pandemic to connect individuals and provide social support despite the physical distance. Older individuals, including those in nursing homes and some with dementia often barred from having visitors, have reduced isolation and loneliness when connected to others through videoconferencing. Frontline health-care workers can benefit from support groups via videoconferencing and telephone. Individuals suffering from COVID-19 have been connected virtually to their loved ones in order to communicate and even to say final goodbyes in some cases.

CHURCH ONLINE

The religious use of technology soared in the early days of the global coronavirus pandemic. Stay-at-home orders, physical distancing recommendations, and quarantine restrictions prompted many worshiping communities to use technology in new ways. With stunning rapidity, congregations installed cameras, aimed them at the altar, and began streaming worship services online. Almost overnight, congregations moved to conducting worship over video-meeting platforms, FM transmitters, websites, or social media. While it might have taken a congregation years to act under normal circumstances, the exigencies of the COVID-19 pandemic meant worshiping communities had to engage new media and technologies. And the importance of this fast action cannot be overstated. Gallup's November 2020 health and health-care survey found that frequent church attendance, even virtual, was a protective factor for maintaining mental wellness during the pandemic.[63]

Posting sermon messages online, holding Bible class via teleconference, and emailing church members to stay in touch provided a way for people to hear the Gospel, engage the Word of God, and stay connected as a congregation. Yet this rush to move church online left little room or time for reflecting on some very important questions: How does a worshiping community go about determining which technologies to use for corporate worship and why? Which elements of the worship service can be mediated through digital technology, and which cannot? What are the repercussions, both corporately and individually, of using new media and technology for worship?

A thorough theological examination of these questions is beyond the scope of this epilogue. However, at least one point should be made on this topic. God reveals Himself to us clothed in earthly media. God is a multimedia God, coming to us through the media of Word, Baptism, and the Lord's Supper. As such, we can recognize how internet technologies can communicate some media, but not all media. The Word of God can be proclaimed very easily through a video or audio sermon. The Lord's Supper, on the other hand, cannot. It is possible to move some aspects of church online, but not all aspects.

While the full Gospel can be communicated online, the fullness of the Gospel cannot be. This is not a problem. As we hear in the Smalcald Articles:

> God is superabundantly generous in His grace: First, through the spoken Word, by which the forgiveness of sins is preached in the whole world [Luke 24:45–47]. This is the particular office of the

---

63 Megan Brennan, "Americans' Mental Health Ratings Sink to New Low," Gallup, December 7, 2020, https://news.gallup.com/poll/327311/americans-mental-health-ratings-sink-new -low.aspx.

Gospel. Second, through Baptism. Third, through the holy Sacrament of the Altar. Fourth, through the Power of the Keys. Also through the mutual conversation and consolation of brethren.[64]

Since God is superabundantly generous in His grace, we may receive this grace only through the spoken Word online for a time (during a pandemic) while we await the day when we can gather together in person as a congregation to receive this grace in others ways, such as the Lord's Supper.

RAPID INFORMATION

Social media can also be a form of social communication and support when we use it to share information in healthy ways and promote positive mental health strategies. A mutual sense of awareness of what is going on and how one is feeling, in addition to sharing one's values, are powerful tools to promote wellness. Unfortunately, the COVID-19 pandemic has also caused an infodemic; we experienced a tidal wave of information about the disease, much of it false.

Frequent exposure to this information and seeing the suffering of others can lead to anxiety, feelings of powerlessness, and obsessing about worst-case scenarios. It is possible to take things both too seriously and not seriously enough. Appropriate precautions are not taken when pandemics are reduced to jokes and memes. Ideally, the government would disseminate timely and correct information, and individuals would heed medical advice from properly trained health-care professionals and follow evidence-based, reputable news sources. We also must learn how to critically evaluate information we consume, especially online, as discussed earlier in the book.

---

64 SA III IV 1.

PERSONAL WELLNESS

Positive technologies that may improve personal wellness include apps, virtual reality, and video games, especially when we don't have access to in-person physical wellness programs, social outlets, and stress relief. Apps can offer mental health information, support, and resources. These include instruction on meditation and mindfulness, alternative pleasurable activities, suggested physical activity, self-assessment tools, self-help cognitive behavioral therapy, and even digital counseling. Virtual reality technology has been used for social connectedness and stress management, including support of hospital caregivers. Video games, especially those with in-game socialization, can make individuals feel less stressed and lonely. Say what you will about Fortnite, but many young people would have struggled to make it through the pandemic without it. Other video games, sometimes called exergames, focus on physical exercise and dance. Classic examples are Wii Fit and the Just Dance series. Home exercise equipment, including bikes and mirrors, can be linked to livestreamed exercise classes, which foster a sense of accomplishment and community.

CONCLUSION

Even if only for a time, the COVID-19 pandemic restructured nearly all aspects of daily life, altering the way people work, gather, learn, worship, and play. It also restructured our relationship with the technologies we use on a daily basis. In a short amount of time, digital technology and the internet became vitally important for health, education, spirituality, and socialization.

Despite this tremendous but necessary reliance on

technology during a time of pandemic, the issues presented in the previous chapters of this book still remain. Human beings struggled to use technology with purpose before the COVID-19 pandemic. These struggles became more pronounced in the midst of the pandemic. And we can be certain that they will remain long after the pandemic is over.

Regardless of timing, pandemic or no pandemic, the heart of the matter remains the same: it is disastrous when technology is at the center of our lives. Everything else—our mental, physical, and spiritual health—becomes unbalanced. Technology is not capable of holding all things together. Thanks be to God, there is One who can. When the god of technology is dethroned from the center of our lives, the true God, Father, Son, and Holy Spirit, can assume His rightful place within our hearts and lives.

Redeeming technology depends on the true Redeemer, Jesus Christ, being at the center of our lives. With Christ at the center, technology finds its place.